THE ROCK

The Life And Crimes Of Palmer Rockey

By Cookie Ann Rockey

Edited by Faye Schliep and Chris Carson

Order this book online at www.trafford.com
or email orders@trafford.com

Most Trafford titles are also available at major online book retailers.

© Copyright 2012 Cookie Ann Rockey.

All rights reserved. No part of this publication may be reproduced, stored in a retrieval system, or transmitted, in any form or by any means, electronic, mechanical, photocopying, recording, or otherwise, without the written prior permission of the author.

Printed in the United States of America.

ISBN: 978-1-4669-5020-7 (sc)
ISBN: 978-1-4669-5019-1 (hc)
ISBN: 978-1-4669-5018-4 (e)

Library of Congress Control Number: 2012913798

Trafford rev. 08/09/2012

 www.trafford.com

North America & international
toll-free: 1 888 232 4444 (USA & Canada)
phone: 250 383 6864 ♦ fax: 812 355 4082

CONTENTS

Chapter 1	BEFORE PALMER	1
Chapter 2	MEETING PALMER	8
Chapter 3	TEXAS TWO STEP	22
Chapter 4	LOS ANGELES	26
Chapter 5	GOODBYE TO HOLLYWOOD	33
Chapter 6	BACK TO DALLAS	38
Chapter 7	BACK TO THE CON	42
Chapter 8	A NEW CHAPTER IN LIFE	73
Chapter 9	MY LIFE	77
Chapter 10	BREAKDOWN AND SEPARATION	80
Chapter 11	A NEW BEGINNING	91
Chapter 12	THE FINAL DAYS	95
Chapter 13	THE REAL PALMER ROCKEY	97
Chapter 14	"SCARLET LOVE"—THE PLOT THICKENS	109
	SOME INTERESTING FACTS AND OBSERVATIONS FROM WIKIPEDIA	115

Chapter 1

BEFORE PALMER

It was the fall of 1966, the trees were turning yellow in the Pacific Northwest. Coolness had set in and I was thankful for the change of weather. It had been very uncomfortable at my job during the hot weather. Working outside is not pleasant even on a good day, but I was young, 19 at the time.

I applied for the mail carrier job because I liked the outdoors after carrying the newspaper for my brother in the summers for 4 years and before that I helped him carry on Sundays from the time I was 8 years old. Also, my aunt worked at the Post Office in San Francisco and it was a good job for her.

I had to wait for 3 months and was accepted after passing the Civil Service test. This was my first real job with benefits. I requested to work in Seattle, as I knew I could get on quicker there than in Tacoma where I was born and raised. Also, I wanted to get away from my family restrictions as all young people do. I wanted to be independent, because I knew everything!

The Post Office I worked at was in the University of Washington area. It was really something to see how the students lived in the old houses around the campus. It was the beginning of the Hippie movement and they had no furniture, but sat in circles on the floor. I knew I didn't want that. I got caught one time in a Sorority hazing walk. The girls were talking and pointing at me in my uniform. I knew I didn't want that either. I was glad I was living at the YWCA in downtown Seattle, across the street from the swankiest hotel in the city, The Fairmont.

*   *   *

The YWCA was for women only and they rented out rooms, either with a roommate, or very rarely, a single room. The Young Women's Christian Association was a temporary living place for women who couldn't afford an apartment when they moved to the big city. No men were allowed past the front desk. There was a restaurant adjacent to the Y, as it was called for short. The Y had an Olympic size pool that was open to everyone, who paid for a membership each month or yearly to the YWCA or YMCA (Young Men's Christian Association). There was a separate entrance for men going to the swimming pool.

The Y had a day care, although no children were allowed in the rooms with the women. We were mainly young single women. They still have 116 rooms for women with a 24 hour front desk and secured elevator entry for all floors. Only now, they have a shared bathroom between two rooms and only one woman in each room. Each room has a small refrigerator in it.

Back then, there were communal bathrooms and most rooms were double occupancy.

We had kitchen privileges. The refrigerator had metal wire lock boxes in it. We could only put our food to be refrigerated in the cages as it would be stolen otherwise. Much stealing went on and even with a lock on the cage, if someone could grab something out of the cage, it would be gone. I saw this happen, but the girl, trying to get some bacon out, told me it was her cage; that she lost the key to the padlock. I found out later that the cage belonged to someone else.

I roomed with someone at first, but later when I got a raise, I moved to the biggest single room they had in the old building.

One man accosted me on the street trying to sell me insurance one day, because he had seen my picture in the newspaper for being the first woman carrier in the city of Seattle. I had to enter the YWCA to get rid of him.

*   *   *

I was young and knew I needed a car. My Dad took me to buy a blue and white Ford. I don't know what model or make, but my father worked for a Ford Motor Company, so he was loyal to Ford. The first day I drove it to work, it was towed away because I parked in a 2 hour parking zone. I walked to my brother, Robert's trailer, as he was attending the University of Washington, and he took me home. A man from work told me how to find the car, as I was young and ignorant about towing zones. I bailed the car out and then the next morning it wouldn't start. It was the battery, but I was tired of it already and didn't have the money for a battery at that time. What a headache!! The reality of upkeep had hit me. A car was expensive to park downtown and expensive to take care of.

Dad financed it until it broke down. He took it back home to Tacoma, painted it and made some money selling it. He was a "Body and Fender Man" by trade and worked painting cars on the side.

I rode the bus after that during the day and in the morning I took a cab to work as it was too dangerous on the bus in that area of town. When I wasn't working, I walked everywhere.

I walked to the markets on the Sound, where someone was making bread in the form of turtles, alligators and other animals. It was great fun to see everything there.

At the very beginning of my mail carrying days I dated a boy about my age, named Tracy. We went on a double date with his brother to a Beatles concert at the Seattle Center, where The World's Fair had been. We were so far away from the stage, that the Beatles looked like little stick men. Some people next to us let us use their binoculars several times. It was exciting! I had never been to a concert before.

We were both subs and if I was late, he would come out and help me. We got to ride the bus free if we had a Postal bag over our shoulder. Tracy took me down to the most expensive store in town, Frederick & Nelson, where his mother worked. She wrapped up the articles people bought and it was really crowded there with a Security Guard on duty. I looked at a few prices and almost fainted. I was afraid I might break something with my purse and I would not be able to pay for it, so I held my purse really close. I did meet his mother. I had started working in August, then, he was drafted in September. I didn't know if I would ever see or hear from him again. In the spring, out of the blue, I received a letter from him. I told him I was going to marry someone else.

Then a 45 year old carrier, Gene, asked if I would like to meet his son, who was close to my age. He invited me to go square dancing with his family and I would have to stay overnight because they got finished so late. His wife was very nice to me and I ate supper with them 3 or 4 times and went square dancing with them. His wife got out an old dress of hers and modified it so I could wear it. He was an unassigned carrier and was always trying to get me to go somewhere with him during work. I went one time and he tried to kiss me and I knew something was really wrong with this situation. I should have cut off contact with him and his family right then because the next time at breakfast his wife started accusing me of having an affair with him. She told me he was 45, had kids, and she would take everything they had. I didn't know what to say. I was scared to death. I was only 19 and just wanted to run. She kept on by saying that she had seen him get up really early and come in and stare at me for 15 minutes before he woke me up in the morning and he seemed to be in love with me. I turned redder and redder and started to cry.

We left and when I got to work I told him not to talk to me again. Then, Gene stalked me and showed up on my route, at the very end, and asked to drive me back to the station. I told him, "NO!" I finally noticed, the next day, that he was parked on the top of the hill, in the graveyard above the last street of my route. I went in and told my supervisor and he spoke to Gene, because that stopped. Then he showed up when I went for a walk, out of the YWCA. I told him to get lost and he kept walking and talking and I had to run back into the Y to get rid of him. I had to go to the supervisor again and then he stopped.

I was so upset over these events, I had to go to the doctor and get a tranquilizer. The tranquilizer worked.

Then I got my first CREDIT CARDS; something unheard of before this time in my family. Credit Cards were just coming in as a way to shop at your favorite store. My parents signed for a credit card for me at JC Penney's and I was very inept at figuring the bills from the Credit Card, because we received the bill with the holes in the cards, and no one had calculators then. We had to add each purchase separately, but I always had enough money to pay the bill.

Bank statements were also Greek to me and I had no one to help me figure it out. At that time, it cost 10 cents to write a check, so you had to add that cost in every time you wrote one. I dealt in cash most of the time because of bank fees for checks and accounts. But I was able to cash my check at the bank for nothing.

All these experiences in learning about living on your own helped me with Palm as he didn't know much about banking, either. He dealt in cash only, but credit cards were to play an important part in Palmer's life in the future.

Chapter 2

MEETING PALMER

I first met Palmer at the Seattle Public Library. He was confident and dashing. Over the years, many people came in contact with him but none came to know him like I did. How did I get selected to be his confidant you may ask? I was naïve and young, with no friends or relatives in town to object to him. I was on my own.

The library was very close to the YWCA and I loved visiting it. It had more books than any library I had been in.

I was looking up phone numbers in the telephone book section one day, but Palmer must have been looking for a sucker. He was hanging around and struck up a conversation with me. He was middle aged, but looked in his 30's and was very handsome. As I said before, the hippie movement was just beginning. The neighborhood was full of people turning away from the way their parents had dressed and acted. My father wasn't a hippie. He was of the working class and rarely wore a suit. But here was Palmer wearing a suit and tie! That impressed me. His short hair slicked back and curly on top, bowled me over. His hands were not callused, so I thought he was a businessman. I should have known better, since it was during work hours and only the unemployed wandered around at that time. Being young has its disadvantages, mainly no worldly experience about certain types of men and their wiles.

We went to an area where there were chairs and he asked what kind of job I had. I was reluctant to tell him, but proud that I had my picture on the front page of the Seattle Post Intelligencer, just a few weeks before. I was the first woman mail carrier in Seattle. I thought he might know who I was.

I told him to guess my occupation. He asked to look at my hands and guessed the usual—secretary, office worker. Finally, I told him a mail carrier. He acted very mysterious about what he did for a living and even his name was different. I had never heard the name of Rockey before. I liked the sound of it and became fascinated with him. I was young and without friends in the area, to help me get a grip on the situation properly. I know now that anyone who is secretive and old, must have something to hide.

He finally asked me for a date to a nice restaurant. I was under the drinking age, but got by with it because he was older and I looked older than my age. I usually drank Irish coffee. We went out several times, but he would never say where he lived, what he did for a living, or his age.

He talked, all the time, about Jesus. He had been a Catholic and had started reading the Bible. He came around to being saved. For those, who don't know what this means, here is an explanation. Being saved means that you have had a personal conviction that you are a sinner and Jesus died to make you sinless in his Father's eyes. Your sins are forgiven forever and now you are to change your life to obey the 10 commandments. This is summed up in the quote from scripture: "If you confess with your lips that Jesus is Lord, and believe in your heart that God raised him from the dead, you will be saved." (Romans 10:9) A personal relationship with Jesus is the only way you can even try to do that. When you fall out of the relationship, you are backslidden; which happened to Palmer.

His arguments and quoting the Bible impressed me. Then he told me he was a PhD and I was hooked. I couldn't believe he was interested in me and had been a University Professor.

That is when I knew I loved him!

He bought me my first bible for Christmas (1966). I began reading the Bible so I would understand what he was talking about. We went to a different Protestant Church every Sunday. He was so paranoid that he picked me up a block away. I would walk through the lobby of the Fairmont Hotel, which was across the street from the Y, and walk to the door on the other side of the hotel. I should have known that something was wrong with this picture. It added to his allure.

Shortly after our first date, I made some chocolate chip cookies; tons of them. I wanted to show him I could cook. I was trying to impress him. We both got tired of eating them, but he called me "Cookie" after that. The next kind of cookie I tried was sugar cookies. He must not have liked them, because he gave them back to me and told me to ask if the Nursery in the Y could use them. They also told me not to make any more. I got the message.

I like soft cookies and the kids must have made a mess with them. But Cookie stuck and several times he called me that, when he could not remember my real name. That was when he introduced me to someone at a church.

* * *

Palmer finally asked me to support him as a missionary. He was going to make a "life of Christ" that would sweep the world and he would be the Producer, Director, Writer and Star of it. We would be rich and famous.

I met Palm in October and by March he asked me to support him. I ended up paying his rent and giving him spending money for food, gas for his car, and going out after church on Sunday. I did this so he would not have to work as a busboy at a local restaurant at night. He was working there, because he didn't have to use his SS number for that job. He didn't want his backers to know he would stoop that low. (The real truth was, that his Aunt, who he owed money to, for a trip to London, was looking for him.)

When Palm was going to get the first payment from me to support him, we met down the street from the Y, in his old "54 Chevrolet Belaire. Like a stupid fool, I told him how much money I had in the bank and he was going to tell me how much he needed that day. Well, I had just gotten my Income Tax back, in the meantime, and I had more in the bank than I had previously told him. Palm got mad that I hadn't told him the right amount and I had to explain. I forget how much I gave him every 2 weeks, but we had $20 to spend each weekend. I was earning $2.64 an hour at that time. One time we spent $20 on junk food. When he realized that, he said we would have to cut back on snacks. He was the one who bought the stuff, not me.

One night Palm took me out so we could make-out. We parked not far from the Y, on the side of the street, between two parked cars and on a hill (all of downtown Seattle, is on hills). We were kissing for a short time, when some men ran out of a car parked in the parking lot right across the sidewalk from us. They showed us their police badges and told him to get out of the car. One man stayed and questioned me. He took my license back to their car. Palm was with the other policeman and his license was being checked out. I was told that they were plain clothes officers staked out in this district because there had been several rapes in that area. Palm ran back to me and was afraid I had seen his birth date. He was upset that I might know his age. Another sign I ignored. We were let go and told to go somewhere else to neck.

Palm decided to show me where he lived, after that. Palm lived in a run-down hotel at the edge of downtown with many retired people. The hotel was not far from the YWCA and the library. I remember getting in an elevator in his hotel and he looked around for something up above. He said, "In the end they will have cameras in the elevators." That was 45 years ago. I wonder when they put surveillance cameras in elevators? (I think it might have been in the 1980's because that is when the modern elevators were installed in most buildings. In large cities, they have had to put them in first, because of violence.) It was Orwellian at the time, but I didn't catch onto his paranoia.

The room didn't have a bathroom but it did have a sink. The bathroom was communal and down the hall. The bath tubs were in the basement in little cubicles. We went through there several times, and there was always someone taking a bath. It seemed quite dangerous to me. There were no locks anywhere on the cubicles. I couldn't figure out why he wanted to go out the back door into an alley, but soon found out why he skulked around.

His uncle was looking for him so he would have to pay his wife back for the money he borrowed from her.

Shortly thereafter, there was a fire on his floor. He packed his belongings into his suitcase and ran out into the hallway. The smoke was thick and he could hardly see where he was going. He knocked on doors as he headed for the stairs. It was put out and he moved back into a blackened room. Another time he was asleep at night when someone put a key in the lock and a woman opened the door. She was told the room was empty, apologized and left. What a dumpy life. He was a real itinerant. He had an old '54 Chevy and that large suitcase.

One night he opened up to me about his education and serving in the military, as all young men at that time had to serve.

He said, on one date, "I was drafted after WW II and was in the occupation of Germany. While I was there, I learned German from the widow of a German Officer." He told me.

Palm said, "VD was rampant then and they had to show all of the army men what it looked like, and told them to be careful." He emphasized that he never screwed around with anybody and everyone knew it.

The military gave every soldier a carton of cigarettes every week and he made extra money selling his. He visited several countries during that time, including Italy, especially Naples, the birthplace of his father. He used the money from selling cigarettes to tour Europe.

Palmer never mentioned his early education, but talked extensively about St Louis University.

Palm said another time, "When I was going to St Louis University, I worked as a security guard at a business office at night. I could study, then. No place had air conditioning so the ceiling fans were all they had. When I got there, I had to turn off all the extra fans on my rounds of the offices. I watched to see that no one came in illegally."

(What he didn't tell me is that he attended St Edward's College, a seminary, for 3 years and Seattle University in Seattle before going to St Louis University. This I found out from his thesis he wrote to graduate from college.)

Palm told me he had a PhD in Philosophy from St Louis University, where he taught as a professor for several years after graduating. While at the University he said he translated a book from German to English. I have the one he translated from German, "Know and Live the Mass", by Dr Pius Parsch.

Palm spoke 8 or 9 languages fluently and could speak and read some in Hebrew. He started by learning an Italian dialect at home (his family spoke a dialect) and English at school. He learned High Italian, then Spanish, Portuguese, French and German. He could speak Latin, a dead language that he first learned in High School and then at St Edward's. He had teachers but studied very hard on his own. (One day some Portuguese missionaries came to First Baptist and he spoke to them in Portuguese.

The woman commented to me, that Palmer spoke without an accent.)

Spanish people always thought he was Spanish and he always helped them. They would ask what the signs in stores meant. Palm translated two books from Spanish to English while at St Louis University; "The Church and Creation" and "The Catholic Church: The Mystical Body of Christ" by Luis Colomer.

He learned the languages by reading the bible in the language he was learning and compared it to the English Revised Version Bible. He had me try it and I couldn't do it. The bible I tried to read was in Spanish, but I didn't know anything about the Spanish language. It made no sense to me. He taught me a few words in Spanish, but that didn't help because everything was backward from English.

Palm also opened up about his girlfriend in St Louis, whom he broke up with because she was getting serious. She came from a rich family. She bought dresses in the $200 & $300 range in the 50's. That was really expensive back then. He said he didn't know that he was on the same party line as she was and he heard her talking to her girlfriend about the fact that she would marry him in a minute. She didn't know why he didn't call her anymore. He arranged a meeting with her to explain that he could not afford to support her in the way she lived, on his salary. (I guess this was a lesson not to ask for money. But I was earning it, not him.)

Palmer told me he got tired of teaching and decided to go to Med School and all the things that went on there with the students helping each other with all their tests, so they would pass. Palm was not a player and got low grades, so he quit.

That is when he went to Hollywood to make it big in the movies.

Palm told me he had directed a black and white "B" movie, shortly after 1956—he also starred in it. His best friend, who he met in Actors' School, co-starred in it. Ron DiSalvo was his name.

Ron was in the insurance business and lived on a boat in a fashionable marina. He had built a beautiful wood, winding staircase from the bottom floor to the top and it was used in several movies and TV shows. He did the remodeling of the boat as therapy, but it was really a place to live, when he got a divorce.

When Palm "got religion", he took the movie, except two rolls of film, to the city dump and by now it is buried in the land fill. His best friend, Ron who had not made another film, had the two rolls of film. (Ron sent one to him in '71 when he was going to include it in his new film, "It Happened One Weekend".)

Palmer also knew Tom Laughlin from his actor's school days. And spoke extensively about him. It was a long time from the time Palm talked about Tom having a movie about the character of BILLY JACK and when the movie came out. We went to see it. Palmer couldn't believe that he let his wife play the female lead, because she was raped in the picture, and it was pretty graphic.

After Palm couldn't find a distributor for the black and white film, Palmer tried writing scripts for Horror Stars, like Boris Karloff. Palm told me about his stay in England trying to raise money for the black and white film made in the mid 1950's. He had borrowed the money from his Aunt Mary for that trip.

According to an article in the newspaper when his "Scarlet Love" came out, Palmer mentioned that a script was bought by Shepparton Studio for Boris Karloff, but Palm never knew if it was ever made into a film by Boris.

He had started to date a British girl. I don't know why I didn't get mad about him talking about other girls he dated. He had to leave England when he suddenly ran out of money, so he didn't tell her he was leaving.

In the mid 1960's, Palm moved back to his Grandmother's house. I don't know how long he lived there, but it was long enough to wear out his welcome. When he started cashing his Grandmother's Social Security check that was the last straw for his family. He said his Grandmother would wander through the house yelling and crying. He finally grabbed her and told the devil to leave her alone. She never did that again.

This was his Mother's side of the family. His Grandpa was dead at this time. His Mother's sister, Mary, the Aunt who loaned him the money, was asking for it. He would not go out and get a job because he had to be at home to answer the phone when investors from Seattle called. He was trying to get investors for his Life of Christ even then. He said he had to leave the house one day and an investor called. His Grandmother answered, but she didn't speak English, so couldn't take a message. He found this out later by calling the investor back.

He took care of his Grandmother until she died at 92 in 1966. She passed away in Palmer's arms. Palm was supposed to have strained his back lifting her so much.

Palm told me about another time that he was really hungry when the food ran out at his Grandmother's house and he asked a neighbor to give him some food and she wouldn't. I should have figured out, that there was something seriously wrong with him for not going to work before this happened, but I was in love.

Then he told me his Aunts were trying to get him out of the house, after their mother died. They brought him a baggie of lettuce. He figured it had poison on it and threw it away. He never told me how they got him out of the house.

He finally got a job busing tables at a restaurant and moved into a run-down hotel. When you got a job at a restaurant, you could get two free meals a day. This was common at this time. It was like that, so the employer could pay you next to nothing.

* * *

We met in October and I was saved in Central Baptist Church in March of 1967. We would split up for Sunday school and witness to those in the Bible classes, in all different denominations of churches. This way, I saw how all of them operated.

It was very exciting. We would go somewhere afterward and spend all day together. Oh, new love, it blots out good judgment.

Then when we got serious, Palmer convinced me that it would look bad for me to be a mail carrier instead of working inside as a clerk when we got famous. We would also have children and friends when we got famous, not before. Then he asked me to support him in his quest for the money for the life of Christ. By then I was taken in by his knowledge of the Bible and his knowledge of the motion picture industry. I sure was naive. I thought I had been saved and this was my work. I would follow him anywhere! Oh, new love! I could live out of a suitcase just for Jesus, but it turned out to be for Palmer.

I put in for a transfer to clerk, through the supervisor, giving as my reason "my back was being strained by carrying the pouch every day for 6 days". I transferred January 1st of 1967 to the Terminal Annex by the Train Station. The mail went by train then, for the most part, as Air Mail was extra.

* * *

During that time, I was alienated from my family. I attended 1 year of college. I decided to get a job instead of going to college, but always with the intention of going back to college. I had to be on my own.

Palmer insisted I not discuss Palm with my family. No wonder! He was 25 years older than me.

Just before we left Seattle, he was sued for the money he owed his Aunt Mary. That was when one of his many relatives in the area, saw him walking downtown near where he lived and followed him to his hotel. He had to sign over his share in his Grandmother's estate to get rid of the lawsuit.

I should have noticed that he lived with women or off their money.

Palm signed over his car to me and I never knew why for sure, but it must have been that he owed enough money to his relatives, so that they could take his car, also. His reason was that it would be better if I had the car in my name.

Chapter 3

TEXAS TWO STEP

Palm wanted to go to Dallas, Texas because he had heard, from reading at the library, that there were many rich people to present his film to in Dallas. One was Robert LeTourneau, of LeTourneau University fame. Palm found a book on his life in the library in Seattle and found that LeTourneau gave 90% of his income from inventing heavy equipment to the University. RG was a prolific inventor of earthmoving equipment. He had 300 patents. 70% of earthmoving machinery during WW II was invented by Le Tourneau. The University was founded by RG and his wife, Evelyn, and sits where Harmon General Hospital used to be. It was first called LeTourneau Technical Institute. RG was the first person Palmer went to see, when he landed in Dallas. He took a bus from Dallas to Longview to see RG. Palm also met RG's son, Richard, who was in charge of the business at the time. Palm was looking for some of the 90% to be donated to his Life of Christ, but RG died 2 years after Palm met him.

He also found that HL Hunt was a Christian and lived in Dallas. HL was the richest man in the world at that time. He was semi-retired at the time and ate lunch in his office. In other words, he brown-bagged it. Palmer caught him at that time and probably talked him to death. He never invested any money in Palmer's film project.

We found that HL Hunt's daughter was a member of the church we eventually joined and in charge of the teen programs. (She also was hit up for money.)

He had also heard of W. A. Criswell, the head of the First Baptist Church of Dallas. Criswell was a great preacher and had the largest congregation of Southern Baptists in the world—26,000 members. (And Criswell should read his script.) Criswell was conservative and evangelical. Billy Graham was counted among the members since 1953-2008 and was a close friend of the Criswells.

I got a transfer from Seattle to Dallas with the Post Office. I left without a word to my family. I did not contact them during my marriage. He told me when he asked me to marry him that I would have to choose between my family and him. I was in love and found it fascinating to leave where I was born and raised, and travel to Texas.

We joined Criswell's church when we arrived in Dallas and were baptized by Criswell in March of 1968. We were married by W. A. Criswell in his study, in June of 1968. I was 21. Palm was trying to get a letter from Criswell saying the script was great. Palm asked him to read his script and Criswell did. But when he got a letter from him it was one sentence long and very non-committal. No personal signature, either. Palm couldn't use it to raise money and Criswell must have known that.

* * *

We lived separately until we were married and then moved to an apartment on Live Oak Street in Dallas, not far from downtown. It was owned by HL Hunt's daughter.

After we were married, I found out some of his quirks:

I learned quickly that you don't wake him up by shaking him or even touching him, unless you wanted to be in a death grip. I wondered all the time about what must have gone on for him to be like that.

He had weird ways about him. I found he used lifts in his shoes to make himself taller. He used black Pomade to fill in where he had lost hair and his hair was white, under the Pomade. He had to have nice sport coats and suits for visiting. At one point, I caught him wearing my black Spanish broad-brimmed hat and looking at himself in a mirror, from every side. He was different, for sure!

He wanted me to tell no one about myself and especially nothing about him. Silence was stressed. I also learned, I was not to speak in front of other men. And never express an opinion that differed from his.

I was always told, we would be rich and have lots of friends, then, and who they would be. We looked at a mansion on Swiss Avenue that was being remodeled to sell. We looked at a new house and I dreamed!

Palmer referred to himself as "The Rock". I don't know why except maybe he was called that as a kid. He was in love with himself!

Palm told me one day, about an incident that happened to him in a restaurant he was eating in the day before. A woman near him looked very concerned and was by herself. He asked her, if she wanted to talk to him and they took a walk outside. She had been contemplating suicide because of her situation.

Palm talked her out of it with some great advice and she decided she would try to figure a way out of her situation. Years later he met her there, again, to hit her up for money sources, for his script on the Life of Christ.

She was happy at that time. He got no money from her or sources.

Chapter 4

LOS ANGELES

We made no headway on raising money in Texas, so Palm decided to suddenly move to LA. It was after he started a stink with the utility man at our apartment house in Texas. He had caught the utility man looking at me through a small window by the kitchen table. It got ugly and we left overnight. He only had a '54 Chevrolet and we had to carry all our belongings in it. We left in the darkness. I remember being scared, because I was afraid of the dark. I had applied for a transfer to LA Terminal Annex on the LSM machines, just like I had operated in Seattle for several years. Dallas didn't have them yet. I only stayed in Dallas 11 months and left them without telling any employees I was transferring. I didn't tell the employees my name had changed when I got married, either and I was not to answer questions people asked about my personal life. I was scared I would not obey him properly. I didn't realize—"How would he know what I said at work? unless I was stupid enough to tell him. And I was."

I didn't realize that that was his paranoia and how he kept me under his thumb!

*   *   *

In LA, I had transferred with no break in service and worked at the Terminal Annex. I was a wiz on the machines, but again was a loner. Palmer didn't want me to have friends anywhere until we were famous, which would be soon. He kept telling me the same song and dance, every chance he got, to keep me from getting discouraged. I became very depressed in LA and just sat around.

I did bible study because that was the only book I was allowed to read. We practiced his lines from the script every day, so he would be ready to step into the character of Jesus as soon as he got the money to make the film. He even took lessons from a Rabbi to learn Hebrew. I made him a garment like Jesus wore in pictures and he bought a moustache and beard and had his picture taken professionally in that get-up. I did the retyping of the script when he changed it from a three hour movie to 1 ½ hour one. I hand printed a list of what props were needed for each scene, as instructed by Palm. Each scene had it's own square on the paper, with all the props needed for that scene in the square. It was tedious doing it, but I did it out of love.

We lived in a one bedroom apartment in Burbank, across from Columbia Ranch. Many popular TV shows were filmed there, especially westerns and The Flying Nun, that catapulted Sally Fields to stardom. Columbia Ranch occupied an entire block. This was a working class neighborhood. I dreamed of living in Beverly Hills, not The Valley! How Palmer thought living here would make an impression on anybody in Hollywood, I don't know!

Our neighbors were workers at Columbia Ranch. The Ranch burned twice in two years and the smoke drove us outside to watch. On the most recent occasion, the smoke poured in the open window of our bedroom, where I was sleeping. It was not warm enough to have the air conditioner on. We heard later that someone threw Molotov Cocktails over the wall of Columbia Ranch. The cocktails were easy to make and easy to hide in clothing while walking by the Ranch. The fire was worse by mid afternoon and the street was closed to traffic. They never caught the culprits, and I kept up with all the news from the newspaper.

One time we watched the filming of "Airport" from the road as they filmed with half the airplane on the Universal Studio lot. It was fascinating. Each day the scene was different and it was really exciting to see the snow falling outside the aircraft in the summer heat. When I saw the movie, I could not see where it was split in half like it was on the lot. It showed me that films are not like the real thing and I have never forgotten that.

One day we watched a scene being shot for Ephraim Zimbalast Jr's TV show (The FBI) in the parking lot of Von's Supermarket not far from the apartment we lived in. We stood behind the script girl and watched what she did. He pointed things out that I hadn't noticed right off hand. (It helped me later as the script girl on "Scarlet Love".)

Also, at another time, we saw several stars—Paul Newman, his wife, Joanne Woodward, in a floppy hat, and family at a horse riding arena. Their young daughter was riding in competition at the time. They were all in their English riding suits. We went there quite often to walk. Eva Gabor got out of a car just behind us one time. Rock Hudson rode a young horse in a competition. The young horse made him look inexperienced as a rider. The commoners criticized him the whole time. Palmer was thinking of going to the stars for money.

Then we went on vacation to San Diego. What a trip, or should I say it was a TRIP! We got down there about noon and it was cold to me so I laid on a chaise lounge with my brown coat on. Some girls were talking excitedly several feet away and one approached me and asked for my autograph. I didn't know who I was supposed to be. I asked her who she thought I was, but I didn't know the person she thought I was (Miss Snow). I declined to autograph her paper. She was really disappointed. (Miss Snow was again mentioned on a bus I was riding in LA. I was wearing my hair pulled back at the nape of my neck and wore a brown coat. The same outfit as at the beach. The only Miss Snow at the time was a Mexican lady playing Miss Snow in a Broadway play in LA in Spanish.) I didn't know what to do so we left the beach area. I had to sleep sometime as I slept during the day because of my job. We went to the hotel and I crashed. I suddenly awoke to a commotion on the TV. The astronauts were in trouble and for the rest of the 3 days of vacation that's all that was on TV. A movie was made out of their ordeal—Apollo 13. The space ship was fixed and landed safely.

On the way back, we ran into a road block not far from Los Angeles looking for illegal aliens, etc. The etc. is what I should have been worried about. Wouldn't you know, Palm left his driver's license in, of all places, the trunk of the car; so, before we reached the road block, he pulled over and searched the trunk. This was during the beginning of rampant drug use. As soon as he got back in the car, we were pulled over by some cops and hauled off to a makeshift office where they separated us. Palm looked Mexican anyway, so they really interrogated us. It took more than an hour of questioning and they searched the car and ground around where we stopped, to convince them that we weren't drug pushers, or addicts. Or that he wasn't illegal. I kept saying to myself. "Why does this always happen with this man?"

Palm did better at getting agents to read his script in LA, but he wouldn't give up his desire to direct and star in it. He came so close several times. He went for an interview with a director, who wanted the "woman at the well" to wash her hair as Jesus approached. That told him to turn the director down, as it wasn't scriptural. Another agent wanted to have his client, a producer, buy his script from him. He would not hear of that. The agent sent the script back by a messenger, probably to see where we lived. I was really disappointed!

I worked 10pm to 6:30am and slept until 4pm every day whether I was working or not. It became difficult to go to church with him and he started going by himself and told me all about witnessing in each Bible Class he attended. Not one pastor was interested in his script. No one at the churches he attended was a possible person to extract money from.

Palm flew to visit several rich people including the Billy Graham organization. Not too long afterward, Billy Graham's ministry came out with something similar about Jesus' life. We figured they got the idea from Palm's script.

He flew several places to talk to wealthy Christians and according to him, he saw them. He always brought me back a piece of jewelry.

We did get involved with Amway for awhile, thinking that it was good to associate with these people, but soon found it was a waste of time and money. They were too smart to invest in his film.

The apartment was a great place to live until we started seeing needles everywhere and then came unemployment at Lockheed. People were chaining their cars to telephone poles.

Chapter 5

GOODBYE TO HOLLYWOOD

The reason to go back to Dallas was when the big earthquake of 1971 hit.

That's a story in itself:

It was spring and I had stayed up all night on my one vacation day off during the week. I had been reading and looked up and noticed the dawning was early that morning, much earlier than the last weekend. It was eerily quiet—no bugs or birds making a noise. I wondered why, but went back to reading. Then the rumblings came and the reeling. I ran to the hallway and stood in the doorway, like I was taught to do from a child. Everything was crashing around me (the lamps fell over, things fell off the shelves and then the dishes began to fall out of the cupboards.) I screamed as the sound like water rushing came to my attention. It didn't last long but it seemed like an eternity. Palm was sleeping and when he woke up, he fell out of the bed, trying to run toward the doorway where I was.

When it was over, my heart was beating fast and I was shaking. We surveyed the damage. Water was flowing out of the bathroom into the hallway. The commode had overflowed. No cracks in the walls, thank heavens. But, now I understood why the cupboards had those very difficult magnetic latches on them—to prevent earthquakes from opening them! Our apartment was a disaster. We knew from growing up in an earthquake area, that there was going to be another earthquake, almost as bad as that first one, before the quakes would eventually stop for awhile. We had many quakes, it seemed every few minutes for that first hour, but the big one did not come for two weeks.

Palm and I got dressed and went out to survey the damage as the electricity was out. It was hot in the apartment with no air. We met other people who were looking over the damage also. Electrical transformers were exploding on the poles and there were fires in places. I realized where the rushing water sound came from—it was the pool in the courtyard of the apartment. It looked like some of the water might have gone under the doors on the bottom floor. We were on the 2nd floor.

When I got to work the next day, I realized how fortunate I was to have taken off that night.

My coworkers were abuzz with the stupidity of the Safety Instructions for late night employees. They were all supposed to go down one staircase, in case of a disaster. It was too crowded and women were yelling and screaming and causing all kinds of holdups as they panicked. They stopped to hold onto the railing—refusing to move. It was utter chaos. The old building separated from the new one and no one could cross over from the old to the new. Planks had to be put over the opening for us to walk to work. All the walls had cracked plaster. I learned that the PO did not have to obey the building codes for earthquake safety measures because they were a Federal Building. The Post Office quickly came up to date on the building codes. It took months to repair the damage. After that, we had many fire drills.

Every night afterward, when a quake would come, we would jump up and be ready to get under our cases in front of us. We placed the mail in slots in those cases. On the machines, we didn't feel it as much.

That first night, when the sacks went down the chutes from the 4th floor to the 1st at 3 am for the dispatch, there was a panicky feeling and all talking stopped. We all jumped under our cases. Then someone yelled out "Dispatch!" We all got up with a sigh of relief.

(At that time the mail was sacked into number 3 sacks (small ones) and then tied up. Quite a few sacks were put in larger sacks to be delivered to the carriers at each station for delivery the next day. Also parcels were thrown in large canvas bags for the carriers. So when the dispatch time came the bags were pulled, closed and thrown down the chutes to the waiting trucks.)

Palmer's paranoia returns.

We lived on the second floor in the apartment house. The police were called because a neighbor girl, 7, spit at him as they passed on the stairs. (She just visited her father on weekends.) That was somehow resolved with the police.

I did not know the details, as I only heard Palmer's side of the story. There was no arrest or jail mentioned.

The second time the police were called by a woman. The police woke me up and asked if I knew my husband was standing in front of his picture window in his underwear. I didn't know what to say. He promised to not do it again and we bought thick curtains. We left for Dallas shortly after that.

I got a transfer back to Dallas, but would have to wait 2 months. Palm went on ahead and got an apartment and I stayed in a woman's boarding house in LA. I took a bus home from work and a cab to work at night. The 1971 earthquake had just happened and there was damage everywhere. The women's boarding house was being earthquake proofed, as it had been damaged extensively. For those outside earthquake territory, all new buildings have the earthquake proof codes in them and the older ones didn't have to have them. The building was very old.

I rewrote the scheme to Dallas like they taught LA's scheme. Dallas's scheme was 10 pages long and mine was 4. (Schemes at the PO were how the mail was worked to each carrier for delivery.) I passed the scheme on the machine going 55 letters per minute in 2 weeks on my own time. I got to Dallas on a 2 week vacation and practiced 4 hours a day.

(LSM machines, that I started working on in Seattle in 1966, 6 months after they first put them in, have been fazed-out. I worked on them in Dallas and LA and they were fazed-out after 34 years of service, in 2000.)

Chapter 6

BACK TO DALLAS

Palmer rode the bus back to LA around Thanksgiving, picked up the car at the storage area, where he had stored it for several months. Unfortunately he did not know enough about cars to drain the oil out of the car before storage, and put it back in before taking off to Texas.

Deming, New Mexico. Our car broke down beside the road near Deming around Thanksgiving on our way moving from California back to Dallas. It was cold and windy. The car ran out of oil and was smoking. It ruined the engine.

A car stopped behind us and there were 2 drunk men, a drunk woman, a young boy and a young girl in it. I was out of the car and near theirs' when I got in the way of the woman jumping out the passenger side to keep one of the men from finding what she threw out the window. They were dressed like cowboys and Palm was dressed like a business man, but they thought he was a hippie-type from his hair. Palm was out trying to flag someone down to take us to the nearest town. His hair was very curly, but when the wind got a hold of his hair, it looked long. Somehow I heard one of them say something about a gun and I ran back to our car. Another car stopped just then and took him to town after getting the drunks to drive off.

When Palm found someone to haul our car to town, he returned and we rode in the wrecker to the garage. Always with Palm, it was dangerous. He was an angry guy and the mechanics were circling us at the garage, when we arrived in Deming. One said, "You better not be trying to take us to the cleaners." I didn't understand what that was all about and Palm never would explain. He must have said something when he first got there that pissed them off, as usual. We finally got it settled that they would put an engine in for a certain amount of money, probably twice as much as somewhere else.

We stayed in a fleabag hotel and left on the bus the next day. The bus took all night to get to Dallas and there were some really wild characters on the bus. Just listening to their conversations was enough to scare you. I could not go to the bathroom even once. The bus' bathroom stunk to high heaven.

*   *   *

Back to the Post Office, back to work.

Shortly after I returned to Dallas, I began to work on the machines.

One employee I worked with was an older man named, John, who had many years at the Post Office under his belt. He was a dirty old man and ogled all the young women. He made several passes at me, even though he was married. One time he came up to me and ran into me full force. He almost knocked me down. I was afraid and ran off. After that he began following me in the building. I noticed he was going out of the building at lunch and coming back high. He quickly escalated to acting crazy.

After work one night, he drove up in his "bug" and opened the door for me to get in. Palm was due to pick me up any minute in front of the Terminal Annex. I stood inside the doors. When John slammed the door and started walking toward me and stared at me with his fists clenched, I ran toward the guard inside. The guard had seen his actions. He told me to tell my husband. When I did, I got really scared because we went to the Postal Inspectors and they said they would keep him away from me. That never happened and he was warned many times, to no avail. Palm did nothing to stop the situation. He was a coward.

Finally, I came into work one Sunday at the Parcel Post Annex. We were not at our regular job. We were working overtime and were told when to go home each night. I found out John had left the building before they announced we were to go home for the night. He came in later and was found working. The supervisor discovered he hadn't clocked out and took John into the office to counsel him, since he had done this before. The supervisor and John got into a fight and John started strangling the supervisor. Thank heaven the microphone to the whole building was on and someone stopped John, just in time. He ran from the building. When I came in Sunday the supervisor told me to watch for John because he tried to strangle him. John didn't show up that Sunday but did Monday, at the Terminal Annex. According to the rules they couldn't put him off the clock because too much time had passed. (John's brother was in management and always got him out of trouble.)I don't know how they got him to rehab, but they did, and he came back to work sober. I was scared the whole time. I was violently ill at first. Attempted murder and no charges were filed? Amazing!! The supervisor, who was almost strangled, quit being a supervisor.

Chapter 7

BACK TO THE CON

Three years before I left Palm, I started working 12 hours a day 6 days a week and 8 hours on Sunday, with no days off. When Palm went out of town, I would take off work, using some of my vacation leave.

Palm never worked at a regular job. I always worked to support him. He handled all the money as he was 25 years older than me. He always had to tell me that he couldn't get a regular job because he was a Producer, Director, Writer and Star.

He visited every office building in Dallas and met most of the movers and shakers in Dallas. We visited OL Nelms, a well known rich man in Dallas, in the hospital. We were thrown out of the Catholic Bishop's office for coming back one too many times. We got married in the Catholic Church trying to get money for the Life of Christ from Catholics. He was trying to raise money our whole marriage to make a 'Life of Christ' his way.

I wrote down all the conversations Palm had with investors because I thought he showed such brilliance in answering their questions and presenting his cause about the "Prince of Peace". He kept all my paperwork on his conversations. I wrote on scraps of paper or torn envelopes. I wonder what happened to all that?

Many businessmen wanted to donate $100 or so but he wouldn't take it. Or so he said.

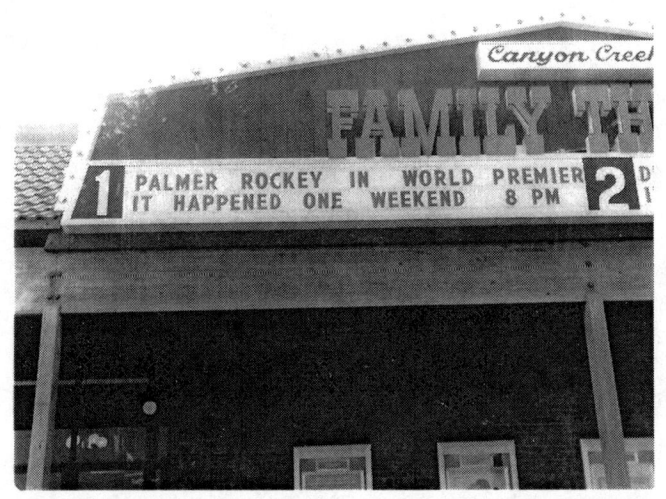

STATE OF WASHINGTON
DEPARTMENT OF HEALTH

MAIL OR DELIVER THIS CERTIFICATE TO YOUR LOCAL REGISTRAR, NOT TO THE STATE BOARD OF HEALTH.

Record No. 5108
Registered No. 5299

PLACE OF BIRTH
County of **King**
City or Town of **Seattle**

Washington State Board of Health
Bureau of Vital Statistics
CERTIFICATE OF BIRTH

Registration Dist. No. _____ (No. **Swedish Hospital** St.; _____ Ward)

FULL NAME OF CHILD: **PALMIERO ROCKEY** (If child is not yet named make supplemental report, as directed.)

Sex of Child: **Male**	Twin, Triplet or other?	Number in order of birth	Legitimate? **Yes**	Date of Birth: **Nov. 17 1921**

FATHER
Full Name: **Joe Rockey**
Residence: ~~[redacted]~~
Color: **White**
Age at last Birthday: **25** (Years)
Birthplace (State or Country): **Italy**
Occupation: **Laborer**

MOTHER
Full Maiden Name: **Jessie Miranti**
Residence: ~~[redacted]~~
Color: **White**
Age at last Birthday: **26** (Years)
Birthplace (State or Country): **Italy**
Occupation: **Housewife**

Number of child of this mother: **1st**
Number of children, this mother, now living: **one**

CERTIFICATE OF ATTENDING PHYSICIAN OR MIDWIFE.*

I hereby certify that I attended the birth of this child, who was {born alive / stillborn} †and that it occurred on **November 17**, 1921, at **9:30** M. **M.** (Signature) **C. L. Templeton, M.D.**

Give name added from a supplemental report: _____
Address: **509 American Buml bldg.**
Filed **Dec. 7**, 19 **21** **H. M. READ**, M. Registrar

† Indicate which by drawing line through superfluous word.

200 JAN 23 1922

STATE OF WASHINGTON
DEPARTMENT OF HEALTH

Washington State Board of Health
BUREAU OF VITAL STATISTICS
CERTIFICATE OF DEATH

Record No. 2468

PLACE OF DEATH
- County of: ......
- City or Town of: ......
- Registration Dist. No.: ...... No. ...... Swedish Hospital
  (If death occurred in a hospital or institution, give its NAME instead of street and number)

Registered No. ......

2. FULL NAME: PALMIRA ROCKY
   - (a) Residence No. ██████████
       (Usual place of abode)
   - (b) If non-resident, give city or town, and state ......
   - (c) How long in Registration Dist. ...... yrs. ...... mos. ...... ds.; how long in U. S., if of foreign birth ...... yrs. ...... mos. ...... ds.

Personal and Statistical Particulars

3. Sex: Female
4. Color or Race: White
5. Single, Married, Widowed or Divorced: Married
5a. If married, widowed, or divorced:
    Husband of or Wife of: Joseph Rocky
6. Date of birth: ...... (Month) ...... (Day) 1894 (Year)
7. Age: 27 yrs. ...... mos. ...... ds. ...... hrs. ...... or min. ...... If less than one day
8. Occupation of deceased:
   (a) Trade, profession, or particular kind of work: Housewife
   (b) General nature of industry, business, or establishment in which employed (or employer): ......
   (c) Name of employer: ......
9. Birthplace (City or town): Italy
   (State or country): ......

PARENTS
10. Name of Father: Angelo Morante
11. Birthplace of Father (City or town): Italy
    (State or Country)
12. Maiden name of Mother: Jessie ---
13. Birthplace of Mother (City or town): Italy
    (State or Country)

14. Informant: Joseph Rocky
    Address: ██████████

15. Filed ...... 19.... A. M. READ, M. D., Registrar.

Medical Certificate of Death

16. Date of death: Nov. (Month) 17 (Day) 1921 (Year)
17. I HEREBY CERTIFY, That I attended deceased from Nov. 1, 192 1 to Nov. 17, 192 1. that I last saw h......r alive on Nov. 17, 192 1, and that death occurred on the date stated above, at 11:50.
    (State the disease causing death, or, in deaths from violent causes, state: (1) Means and nature of injury; and (2) whether ACCIDENTAL, SUICIDAL, or HOMICIDAL).
    The CAUSE OF DEATH was as follows:

    READ DETAILS ON OTHER SIDE
    (Primary) Eclampsia
    (See 1 and 3 other side)   14
    ...... (Duration) ...... yrs. ...... mos. 2 ds.
    CONTRIBUTORY (Secondary) Pregnancy
    (See 2 other side)
    ...... (Duration) ...... yrs. ...... mos. ...... ds.

18. Where was disease contracted if not at the place of death?: ......
    (a) Did an operation precede death? ...... Date of ......
    (b) Was there an autopsy? ......
    (c) What test confirmed diagnosis? ......
    (Signed) C. L. Templeton, M. D.
    11-18, 192 1 Address American Bank Bldg

19. Place of Burial, Cremation or Removal: Calvary   Date of Burial: 11-21-192 1
20. Undertaker: Collins Bros.   Address: ......

I HEREBY CERTIFY, upon honor, that I have made the effort but was unable to secure answers to questions 6
(Insert numbers of unanswered questions)
(Signature of Undertaker) A. A. Collins

DEC 14 1921

Form SS-5
TREASURY DEPARTMENT
Internal Revenue Service
(Revised April 1936)

APPLICATION FOR SOCIAL SECURITY ACCOUNT NUMBER
REQUIRED UNDER CHAPTER 9, SUBCHAPTER A, OF THE INTERNAL REVENUE CODE
(FORMERLY TITLE VIII, SOCIAL SECURITY ACT)

READ INSTRUCTIONS ON BACK BEFORE FILLING IN FORM

EACH ITEM SHOULD BE FILLED IN. IF THE INFORMATION CALLED FOR IN ANY ITEM IS NOT KNOWN, WRITE "UNKNOWN"

PLEASE PRINT WITH INK-OR-USE-TYPEWRITER

1. Rutherford Palmer   Louis   Rockey
   WORKER'S FIRST NAME / MIDDLE NAME (IF YOU HAVE NO MIDDLE NAME, DRAW A LINE) / LAST NAME
   (MARRIED WOMAN—FOR MIDDLE NAME, GIVE LAST NAME BEFORE MARRIAGE; FOR LAST NAME, GIVE HUSBAND'S LAST NAME)

2. FULL NAME UNDER WHICH YOU WORK, IF DIFFERENT FROM NAME SHOWN IN ITEM 1: Rockey Palmer

3. 2206 Eastwood Place   Seattle, Wash.
   WORKER'S PRESENT HOME ADDRESS (STREET AND NUMBER) / (CITY) / (STATE)

4. MARRIED MAN—GIVE WIFE'S FULL NAME BEFORE MARRIAGE: Mary Murphy

5. BUSINESS NAME OF PRESENT EMPLOYER: _____

6. BUSINESS ADDRESS OF PRESENT EMPLOYER (STREET AND NUMBER): _____

7. AGE AT LAST BIRTHDAY: 18   8. DATE OF BIRTH: Nov. 17, 1921   9. PLACE OF BIRTH: 602272 Utah (CITY) _____ (COUNTY) (STATE)

10. FATHER'S FULL NAME: Elbert Rockey   11. MOTHER'S FULL NAME BEFORE MARRIAGE: Jessie Murphy (REGARDLESS OF WHETHER LIVING OR DEAD)

12. SEX: ✓ MALE ___ FEMALE   13. COLOR OR RACE: ___ WHITE ___ NEGRO ___ OTHER ✓ (SPECIFY)

14. HAVE YOU FILLED OUT A CARD LIKE THIS BEFORE? ___ YES ✓ NO — (IF YES, GIVE PLACE AND DATE OF ORIGINAL FILING AND REASON FOR FILING AGAIN)

15. DATE SIGNED: 6-5-40   16. APPLICANT'S (DO NOT PRINT) SIGNATURE: Rutherford Louis Rockey
    (FIRST NAME) (MIDDLE NAME) (LAST NAME)

RETURN COMPLETED APPLICATION TO, OR SECURE INFORMATION ON HOW TO FILL OUT APPLICATION FROM, NEAREST SOCIAL SECURITY BOARD FIELD OFFICE. THE ADDRESS CAN BE OBTAINED FROM LOCAL POST OFFICE.

16—5628

U.S. World War II Army Enlistment Records, 1938-1946 Record

Name:	**Palmer L Rockey**
Birth Year:	1921
Race:	White, citizen
Nativity State or Country:	Washington
State:	Washington
County or City:	King
Enlistment Date:	16 May 1945
Enlistment State:	Washington
Enlistment City:	Fort Lewis
Branch:	No branch assignment
Branch Code:	No branch assignment
Grade:	Private
Grade Code:	Private
Term of Enlistment:	Enlistment for the duration of the War or other emergency, plus six months, subject to the discretion of the President or otherwise according to law
Component:	Selectees (Enlisted Men)
Source:	Civil Life
Education:	4 years of high school
Civil Occupation:	Airplane Fabric And Dope Worker
Marital Status:	Single, without dependents
Height:	00
Weight:	000

Source Information:

National Archives and Records Administration. *U.S. World War II Army Enlistment Records, 1938-1946* [database online]. Provo, Utah: MyFamily.com, Inc., 2005. Original

http://search.ancestry.com/cgi-bin/sse.dll?gsfn=Palmer+L&gsln=Rockey&gsby=1921&gsbco=2%2... 5/7/2006

THE MORAL PHILOSOPHY OF GIAMBATTISTA VICO

by

Palmer L. Rockey, A.M.

Dissertation Presented to the Faculty of the Graduate
School of Saint Louis University in Partial
Fulfillment of the Requirements for the
Degree of Doctor of Philosophy

1955

deborahreynolds
director of member relations

first baptist dallas

1707 san jacinto
dallas, texas 75201
214.969.0111
firstdallas.org

tel 214.969.2402
fax 214.969.7720

May 17, 2006

Name	Carson, Mary Ann	Rockey, Mrs Palmer 10-71 5405 Austin Rd
Address	1414 Bennett	75214 46B #201
	75216 55-K	

Birthday  1946

Date Received by Letter	From What Church Received by Letter	Date Received for Baptism	Date Baptized	Date Dismissed by Letter	Date Dismissed Otherwise
XX		3-10-68	3-10-68		5-10-72 another denom. personal request

To Whom It May Concern:

Mrs. Mary Ann (Carson Rockey) Ashcraft (11/20/46) was baptized at First Baptist Church, Dallas, TX on March 10, 1968

As verified by me, Deborah Reynolds, Church Clerk, First Baptist Dallas, TX.

Deborah Reynolds, Church Clerk
Deborah Reynolds

Texas Marriage Collection, 1814-1909 and 1966-2002 Record

Name:	**Palmer Louis Rockey**
Gender:	Male
Marriage Date:	2 Jun 1968
Estimated Birth Year:	abt 1922
Age:	46
Spouse:	Mary Ann Carson
Spouse Gender:	Female
Spouse Est Birth Year:	abt 1947
Spouse Age:	21
Marriage County:	Dallas
Marriage State:	Texas
Source:	Texas Marriage Index, 1966-2002

Source Information:
Ancestry.com. *Texas Marriage Collection, 1814-1909 and 1966-2002* [database online]. Provo, Utah: MyFamily.com, Inc., 2005. Original data:

- Dodd, Jordan R, et. al. *Early American Marriages: Texas to 1850*. Bountiful, UT: Precision Indexing Publishers, 19xx.

- Hunting For Bears, comp. Texas marriage information taken from county courthouse records. Many of these records were extracted from copies of the original records in microfilm, microfiche, or book format, located at the Family History Library.

- Texas Department of State Health Services. Texas Marriage Index, 1966-2002. Texas Department of State Health Services, Texas.

- Dodd, Jordan, Liahona Research, comp. (P.O. Box 740, Orem, Utah 84059) from county marriage records on microfilm located at the Family History Library in Salt Lake City, Utah, in published books cataloged by the Library of Congress, or from county courthouse records.

A list of counties and year ranges that are included in this database is provided below:

SCHEDULE C (Form 1040) — Profit or (Loss) From Business or Profession
(Sole Proprietorship)
▶ Attach to Form 1040. ▶ Partnerships, joint ventures, etc., must file Form 1065.

1973

Name(s) as shown on Form 1040: PALMER L. + MARY A. ROCKEY

Social security number: [redacted]

A Principal business activity (see Schedule C instructions) ▶ FILM MAKER ; product ▶ FILMS
B Business name ▶ ABBA PRODUCTIONS   C Employer identification number ▶ 75-
D Business address (number and street) ▶ P O BOX 22294
City, State and ZIP code ▶ DALLAS TEXAS 75222
E Indicate method of accounting: (1) ☒ Cash (2) ☐ Accrual (3) ☐ Other ▶
F Were you required to file Form W-3 or Form 1096 for 1973? (See Schedule C Instructions) Yes ☒ No ☐
   If "Yes," where filed ▶ INTERNAL REV. SERVICE AUSTIN, TEXAS
G Was an Employer's Quarterly Federal Tax Return, Form 941, filed for this business for any quarter in 1973? No ☒
H Method of inventory valuation ▶ NA .... Was there any substantial change in the manner of determining quantities, costs, or valuations between the opening and closing inventories? (If "Yes," attach explanation.)

Income
1 Gross receipts or sales $ .... Less: returns and allowances $ .... Balance ▶
2 Less: Cost of goods sold and/or operations (Schedule C-1, line 8) ....
3 Gross profit ....
4 Other income (attach schedule) ....
5 Total income (add lines 3 and 4) 000 00

Deductions
6 Depreciation (explain in Schedule C-3) ....
7 Taxes on business and business property (explain in Schedule C-2) ....
8 Rent on business property .... 900 —
9 Repairs (explain in Schedule C-2) ....
10 Salaries and wages not included on line 3, Schedule C-1 (exclude any paid to yourself) 1513 / 955 48
11 Insurance ....
12 Legal and professional fees ....
13 Commissions ....
14 Amortization (attach statement) ....
15 (a) Pension and profit-sharing plans (see Schedule C Instructions) ....
    (b) Employee benefit programs (see Schedule C Instructions) 42 61
16 Interest on business indebtedness ....
17 Bad debts arising from sales or services ....
18 Depletion ....
19 Other business expenses (specify):
   (a) FILM PROCESSING (35MM-COLOR) 1,564 66
   (b) 5254-EASTMAN KODAK-COLOR-35MM 1,803 90
   (c) FILM PROPERTIES 1,029 50
   (d) CAMERA CARRI - 36MM RENTALS 571 25
   (e) FILM EDITING MACHINES 976 23
   (f) ANSWERING SERVICE 236 68
   (g) FREIGHT EXPENSES 323 47
   (h) BANKING COST (COMMERCIAL CHECKING) 58 11
   (i) FILM LOCATION RENTALS 350 00
   (j) SANGER-HARRIS FINANCE CHARGE 83 59
   (k) Total other business expenses (add lines 19(a) through 19(j)) 6,997 38   10,887 57
20 Total deductions (add lines 6 through 19) 3,898 19   12,785 66

21 Net profit or (loss) (subtract line 20 from line 5). Enter here and on Form 1040, line 28. ALSO enter on Schedule SE, line 5(a) .... ‹12,785 66›

SCHEDULE C-1.—Cost of Goods Sold and/or Operations (See Schedule C Instructions for Line 2)

1 Inventory at beginning of year (if different from last year's closing inventory, attach explanation)
2 Purchases $ .... Less: cost of items withdrawn for personal use $ .... Balance ▶
3 Cost of labor (do not include salary paid to yourself) ....
4 Materials and supplies ....
5 Other costs (attach schedule) ....
6 Total of lines 1 through 5 ....
7 Less: Inventory at end of year ....
8 Cost of goods sold and/or operations. Enter here and on line 2 above ......

Jan. 28, 1974

Internal Revenue Service Center

Austin, Texas 78740

Dear Sirs:

I'm attaching this business expense sheet to my schedule C Form 1040, since I didn't have any room to put them under DEDUCTIONS on schedule C. I'm submitting the entries and giving the total of the attached sheet, which are added to the expenses on schedule C.

My film product will not go on the market until April or May 1974.

Attached sheet expenses for 1973:

1)	Long distance business calls	$ 239.11
2)	PO Box and postage	34.00
3)	Film advertizing	103.25
4)	Business travel costs	611.37
5)	Film screening rentals	65.00
6)	Location and interior stills	149.12
7)	Actor & actress wardrobe	330.00
8)	Xerox copies	141.56
9)	Interest on credit bureau loan	181.78
10)	Free lance film technicians	1,437.00
11)	Interest on Bank loan	38.00
12)	Free lance actors & actresses salary	560.00
		$ 3,890.19

6-18 on schedule C	1,898.09
19(a) -19(j)	6,997.38
attached sheet items	3,890.19
Total	$ 12,785.66 expense

Sincerely,

Palmer J. Rockey

Palmer L. Rockey

SCHEDULE C (Form 1040)
Profit or (Loss) From Business or Profession
(Sole Proprietorship)
Partnerships, Joint Ventures, etc., Must File Form 1065.
▶ Attach to Form 1040.   ▶ See Instructions for Schedule C (Form 1040).

Department of the Treasury — Internal Revenue Service

1974 06

Name(s) as shown on Form 1040: PALMER L. & MARY A. ROCKEY

Social security number: [redacted] 1812

A Principal business activity (see Schedule C Instructions) ▶ FILM MAKER ; product ▶ FILMS
B Business name ▶ ABBA PRODUCTIONS   C Employer identification number ▶ 75-[redacted]
D Business address (number and street) ▶ PO BOX 22294
  City, State and ZIP code ▶ DALLAS TEXAS 75222
E Indicate method of accounting: (1) ☒ Cash (2) ☐ Accrual (3) ☐ Other ▶
F Were you required to file Form W-3 or Form 1096 for 1974? (See Schedule C Instructions.) — No ✓
  If "Yes," where filed ▶
G Was an Employer's Quarterly Federal Tax Return, Form 941, filed for this business for any quarter in 1974? NO
H Method of inventory valuation ▶ NA .... Was there any substantial change in the manner of determining quantities, costs, or valuations between the opening and closing inventories? (If "Yes," attach explanation.) — No ✓

Income
1. Gross receipts or sales $ 696.25 Less: returns and allowances $ .... Balance ▶ 696.25
2. Less: Cost of goods sold and/or operations (Schedule C–1, line 8) ....
3. Gross profit 696.25
4. Other income (attach schedule) ....
5. Total income (add lines 3 and 4) 696.25

Deductions
6. Depreciation (explain in Schedule C–3) ....
7. Taxes on business and business property (explain in Schedule C–2) 31.50
8. Rent on business property 620.00
9. Repairs (explain in Schedule C–2) ....
10. Salaries and wages not included on line 3, Schedule C–1 (exclude any paid to yourself)
11. Insurance ....
12. Legal and professional fees 85.00
13. Commissions ....
14. Amortization (attach statement) ....
15. (a) Pension and profit-sharing plans (see Schedule C Instructions) ....
    (b) Employee benefit programs (see Schedule C Instructions) ....
16. Interest on business indebtedness ....
17. Bad debts arising from sales or services ....
18. Depletion ....
19. Other business expenses (specify):
    (a) ....
    (b) ....
    (c) ....
    (d) See attached sheet ....
    (e) ....
    (f) ....
    (g) ....
    (h) ....
    (i) ....
    (j) ....
    (k) Total other business expenses (add lines 19(a) through 19(j)) 19,297.50
20. Total deductions (add lines 6 through 19) 19,034.00
21. Net profit or (loss) (subtract line 20 from line 5). Enter here and on Form 1040, line 28. ALSO enter on Schedule SE, line 5(a) .... (-18,337.75)

SCHEDULE C–1. — Cost of Goods Sold and/or Operations (See Schedule C Instructions for Line 2)
1. Inventory at beginning of year (if different from last year's closing inventory, attach explanation)
2. Purchases $ .... Less: cost of items withdrawn for personal use $ .... Balance ▶
3. Cost of labor (do not include salary paid to yourself) ....
4. Materials and supplies ....
5. Other costs (attach schedule) ....
6. Total of lines 1 through 5 ....
7. Less: inventory at end of year ....
8. Cost of goods sold and/or operations. Enter here and on line 2 above ....

Jan. 27, 1975

INTERNAL REVENUE SERVICE CENTER
AUSTIN, TEXAS 78740

Dear Sirs:

This is the attached sheet containing 19a of Schedule C.
(Business expenses)

19a)	Newspaper ads	$ 3,663.20
b)	Radio commercials	413.50
c)	Card & poster printing	837.39
d)	Theater rental (2 weeks)	2,000.00
e)	Mixing 35mm sound with 35 mm film	1,878.00
f)	Editing, music, dialogue 35 mm track	1,528.00
g)	Music dubbing session	875.00
h)	Movie titles on 35 mm film	558.90
i)	Processing, printing 35 mm film	2,608.00
j)	Arriflex camera rental	70.00
k)	Banking service charges	108.42
l)	Cameraman	75.00
m)	Car for business operation	109.37
n)	35mm color film negative	144.00
o)	Air freight, shipping film	271.00
p)	Interest on loans	297.43
q)	Miscellaneous	423.64
r)	Postage and box rental	39.34
s)	Search lights for theatre	385.85
t)	Movie rating cost	373.00
u)	Movie screenings	255.00
v)	35mm color stills	109.00
w)	Studio set rental	100.00
x)	Long distance business calls	451.17
y)	Air travel and motel	526.84
z)	Xerox service and copies	192.72
	19a through 19z Total	18,297.50

Sincerely yours,

Palmer J. Rockey
Palmer J. Rockey

NOTIFICATION OF PERSONNEL ACTION
EMPLOYEE, SEE GENERAL INFORMATION ON REVERSE

22

1-NAME (CAPS) LAST-FIRST-MIDDLE	MR.-MISS-MRS.	2-	3-BIRTH DATE (Month, Day, Yr.)	4-SOCIAL SECURITY NO.
ROCKEY PALMER L			11/17/21	

5-VETERAN PREFERENCE	6-TENURE GROUP	7-SERVICE COMP. DATE (For leave)	
1 1-NO 3-10-PT. DISAB. 5-10-PT. OTHER 2-5-PT. 4-10-PT. COMP.	1	09/19/75	

9A-FEGLI	9B-FEGHBP	10-RETIREMENT	11- (For CSC use)
2	3	2 1-CS 3-FS 5-OTHER 2-FICA 4-NONE	

12-NATURE OF ACTION CODE	13-EFFECTIVE DATE (Mo., Day, Yr.)	14-LEGAL AUTHORITY
352 TERMINATION	10/07/75	39 USC 1001

15-FROM: POSITION TITLE	16-PAY PLAN	OCCUPATION CODE	17-LEVEL	STEP	18-SALARY
DISTRIBUTION CLK POSITION NO.	PS	231504XX	05	01	PHS $ 5.63

19-NAME AND LOCATION OF EMPLOYING OFFICE	BLOCK	FINANCE NO.	CLASS	CAG	PAY LOC.	DESIGN	ACTIVITY
POST OFFICE DALLAS , TX 75260		48-2270	1	A			

20-TO: POSITION TITLE	21-PAY PLAN	OCCUPATION CODE	22-LEVEL	STEP	23-SALARY
POSITION NO.					

24-NAME AND LOCATION OF EMPLOYING OFFICE	BLOCK	FINANCE NO.	CLASS	CAG	PAY LOC.	DESIGN	ACTIVITY

25-DUTY STATION (City-State-ZIP Code)	26-GSA LOCATION CODE
DALLAS , TX 75260	481730

27	LEAVE BALANCE	CLASS	ROUTE NO.	TRI-WK.	LENGTH OF ROUTE	L.P. AMT.	STOPS	H.D. HRS.	E.M. ALLOW

30-REMARKS:
☐ A. SUBJECT TO COMPLETION OF _____ PROBATIONARY (OR TRIAL) PERIOD
☐ B. SEPARATION. SHOW REASON BELOW, AS REQUIRED. CHECK IF APPLICABLE:
☐ DURING PROBATION
☐ FROM APPOINTMENT OF 6 MONTHS OR LESS

21
LAST DAY IN PAY STATUS 10/07/75
SF 8 ISSUED
SERVICES NO LONGER REQUIRED

5405 GASTON AVE
DALLAS, TX 75214

31-DATE OF APPOINTMENT AFFIDAVIT (Accessions only)	34-SIGNATURE (Or other authentication) AND TITLE
32-OFFICE MAINTAINING PERSONNEL FOLDER (If different from employing office)	
33-CODE EMPLOYING DEPARTMENT OR AGENCY	35-DATE
PO 02 U.S. POSTAL SERVICE	10/15/75

SCHEDULE SE (Form 1040)
Department of the Treasury
Internal Revenue Service

Computation of Social Security Self-Employment Tax

► Each self-employed person must file a Schedule SE. ► Attach to Form 1040.
► See Earned Income Credit Instructions on page 8 and Instructions for Schedule SE (Form 1040).

1975

- If you had wages, including tips, of $14,100 or more that were subject to social security or railroad retirement taxes, do not fill in this schedule unless you are eligible for the Earned Income Credit. See Instructions.
- If you had more than one business, combine profits and losses from all your businesses and farms on this Schedule SE.

Important.—The self-employment income reported below will be credited to your social security record and used in figuring social security benefits.

NAME OF SELF-EMPLOYED PERSON (AS SHOWN ON SOCIAL SECURITY CARD) | Social security number of self-employed person ►
Palmer L. Rockey

Business activities subject to self-employment tax (grocery store, restaurant, farm, etc.) ► Filmmaker

- If you have only farm income complete Parts I and III. • If you have only nonfarm income complete Parts II and III.
- If you have both farm and nonfarm income complete Parts I, II, and III.

Part I — Computation of Net Earnings from FARM Self-Employment

You may elect to compute your net farm earnings using the OPTIONAL METHOD, line 3, instead of using the Regular Method, line 2, if your gross profits are: (1) $2,400 or less, or (2) more than $2,400 and net profits are less than $1,600. However, lines 1 and 2 must be completed even if you elect to use the FARM OPTIONAL METHOD.

REGULAR METHOD
1 Net profit or (loss) from: (a) Schedule F, line 54 (cash method), or line 74 (accrual method) . . .
(b) Farm partnerships . . . .
2 Net earnings from farm self-employment (add lines 1(a) and (b)) . . . .

FARM OPTIONAL METHOD
3 If gross profits from farming¹ are: (a) Not more than $2,400, enter two-thirds of the gross profits . . .
(b) More than $2,400 and the net farm profit is less than $1,600, enter $1,600 . .

¹ Gross profits from farming are the total gross profits from Schedule F, line 28 (cash method), or line 72 (accrual method), plus the distributive share of gross profits from farm partnerships (Schedule K-1 (Form 1065), line 14) as explained in Instructions for Schedule SE.

4 Enter here and on line 12(a), the amount on line 2, or line 3 if you elect the farm optional method . .

Part II — Computation of Net Earnings from NONFARM Self-Employment

REGULAR METHOD
5 Net profit or (loss) from:
(a) Schedule C, line 21. (Enter combined amount if more than one business.) . . | -20,075 | 84
(b) Partnerships, joint ventures, etc. (other than farming) . . . .
(c) Service as a minister, member of a religious order, or a Christian Science practitioner. (Include rental value of parsonage or rental allowance furnished.) If you filed Form 4361, check here ► ☐ and enter zero on this line . . . .
(d) Service with a foreign government or international organization . . . . . .
(e) Other (See Form 1040 Instructions for line 35.) Specify ► . . . .

6 Total (add lines 5(a) through (e)) . . . . | -20,075 | 84
7 Enter adjustments if any (attach statement) . . . .
8 Adjusted net earnings or (loss) from nonfarm self-employment (line 6, as adjusted by line 7) . . | -20,075 | 84
If line 8 is $1,600 or more OR if you do not elect to use the Nonfarm Optional Method, omit lines 9 through 11 and enter amount from line 8 on line 12(b), Part III.

Note: You may use the nonfarm optional method (line 9 through line 11) only if line 8 is less than $1,600 and less than two-thirds of your gross nonfarm profits,² and you had actual net earnings from self-employment of $400 or more for at least 2 of the 3 following years: 1972, 1973, and 1974. The nonfarm optional method can only be used for 5 taxable years.

NONFARM OPTIONAL METHOD
9 (a) Maximum amount reportable, under both optional methods combined (farm and nonfarm) . . | $1,600 | 00
(b) Enter amount from line 3. (If you did not elect to use the farm optional method, enter zero.) . .
(c) Balance (subtract line 9(b) from line 9(a)) . . . .
10 Enter two-thirds of gross nonfarm profits¹ or $1,600, whichever is smaller . . . . . .
11 Enter here and on line 12(b), the amount on line 9(c) or line 10, whichever is smaller . . . .

² Gross profits from nonfarm business are the total of the gross profits from Schedule C, line 3, plus the distributive share of gross profits from nonfarm partnerships (Schedule K-1 (Form 1065), line 14) as explained in Instructions for Schedule SE. Also, include gross profits from services reported on lines 5(c), (d), and (e), as adjusted by line 7.

Part III — Computation of Social Security Self-Employment Tax

12 Net earnings or (loss): (a) From farming (from line 4) . . . .
(b) From nonfarm (from line 8, or line 11 if you elect to use the Nonfarm Optional Method) . . . | -20,075 | 84
13 Total net earnings or (loss) from self-employment reported on line 12. (If Line 13 is less than $400, you are not subject to self-employment tax. Do not fill in rest of schedule.) . . . . | -20,075 | 84
14 The largest amount of combined wages and self-employment earnings subject to social security or railroad retirement taxes for 1975 is . . . . | $14,100 | 00
15 (a) Total "FICA" wages and "RRTA" compensation . . . . . |
(b) Unreported tips subject to FICA tax from Form 4137, line 9 or to RRTA . .
(c) Total of lines 15(a) and (b) . . . .
16 Balance (subtract line 15(c) from line 14) . . . .
17 Self-employment income—line 13 or 16, whichever is smaller . . . .
18 Self-employment tax. (If line 17 is $14,100.00, enter $1,113.90; if less, multiply the amount on line 17 by .079.) Enter here and on Form 1040, line 59 . . . .

PALMER ROCKEY
P. O. ...
DALLAS, TEXAS 75...

Jan. 27 1976

TO: INTERNAL REVENUE SERVICE CENTER
AUSTIN, TEXAS 78740

Dear Sirs;

This is the attached sheet containing 19a of Schedule C(Business Expenses)

19a)	Developing and printing 35mm film	$3,086.51
b)	Newspaper, TV and Radio advertizing	4,797.56
c)	Theater rental(1 week)	4,000.00
d)	Filming on location	2,371.54
e)	Air travel & motel	1,674.11
f)	Air freight	664.25
g)	Banking service charges	126.82
h)	Postal box rental and postage	63.67
i)	Car for business operations	373.05
j)	Interest on loans	1,123.97
k)	Miscellaneous	488.32
l)	Office supplies	10.74
m)	Film screenings	146.50
n)	Telephone including long distance	757.90
o)	Xerox copies	11.81
p)	Film editing (chem machine)	197.11
q)	Camera supplies	97.68
r)	Storage	104.30
s)	Sync blocks, moviola, splicers	502.03
	TOTAL $	20,597.87

Sincerely,

Palmer J. Rockey
Palmer J. Rockey

SCHEDULE C (Form 1040)
Department of the Treasury
Internal Revenue Service

Profit or (Loss) From Business or Profession
(Sole Proprietorship)
Partnerships, Joint Ventures, etc., Must File Form 1065.
▶ Attach to Form 1040. ▶ See Instructions for Schedule C (Form 1040).

1976

Name of proprietor: PALMER L. + MARY ROCKEY
Social security number: [redacted]

A Principal business activity (see Schedule C Instructions) ▶ FILM MAKER ; product ▶ FILM
B Business name ▶ ABBA PRODUCTIONS   C Employer identification number ▶ 75-[redacted]
D Business address (number and street) ▶ P.C. BOX 22294
City, State and ZIP code ▶ DALLAS, TEXAS 75222

E Indicate method of accounting: (1) ☐ Cash (2) ☐ Accrual (3) ☐ Other ▶ _____ Yes / No
F Were you required to file Form W-3 or Form 1096 for 1976 (see Schedule C Instructions)? . . . . . .
  If "Yes," where filed ▶ _____
G Was an Employer's Quarterly Federal Tax Return, Form 941, filed for this business for any quarter in 1976? NO
H Method of inventory valuation ▶ N.A. Was there any substantial change in the manner of determining quantities, costs, or valuations between the opening and closing inventories? (If "Yes," attach explanation.)

Income
1 Gross receipts or sales $ 7,860.00 Less: returns and allowances $ _____ Balance ▶ 1 7,860 —
2 Less: Cost of goods sold and/or operations (Schedule C-1, line 8) 2
3 Gross profit . . . . 3 7,860 —
4 Other income (attach schedule) 4
5 Total income (add lines 3 and 4) . . . . 5 7,860 —

Deductions
6 Depreciation (explain in Schedule C-3) 6
7 Taxes on business and business property (explain in Schedule C-2) 7
8 Rent on business property 2345 8 Y656
9 Repairs (explain in Schedule C-2) 9
10 Salaries and wages not included on line 3, Schedule C-1 (exclude any paid to yourself) . 10
11 Insurance 11
12 Legal and professional fees 12
13 Commissions 13
14 Amortization (attach statement) 14
15 (a) Pension and profit-sharing plans (see Schedule C Instructions) . . . . . . 15(a)
   (b) Employee benefit programs (see Schedule C Instructions) . . . . (b)
16 Interest on business indebtedness 16
17 Bad debts arising from sales or services 17
18 Depletion 18
19 Other business expenses (specify):
   (a) _____
   (b) _____
   (c) SEE ATTACHED
   (d) SHEET
   (e) _____
   (f) _____
   (g) _____
   (h) _____
   (i) _____
   (j) _____
   (k) Total other business expenses (add lines 19(a) through 19(j)) . . . . 19(k) -54,073 61
20 Total deductions (add lines 6 through 19(k)) . . . . 20 -54,729 61
21 Net profit or (loss) (subtract line 20 from line 5). Enter here and on Form 1040, line 29. ALSO enter on Schedule SE, line 5(a) . . . . 21 -46,869 61

SCHEDULE C-1.—Cost of Goods Sold and/or Operations (See Schedule C Instructions for Line 2)
1 Inventory at beginning of year (if different from last year's closing inventory, attach explanation) . 1
2 Purchases $ _____ Less: cost of items withdrawn for personal use $ _____ Balance ▶ 2
3 Cost of labor (do not include salary paid to yourself) 3
4 Materials and supplies 4
5 Other costs (attach schedule) 5
6 Total of lines 1 through 5 6
7 Less: Inventory at end of year 7
8 Cost of goods sold and/or operations. Enter here and on line 2 above 8

Did you claim a deduction for expenses of an office in your home? . . . . ☐ Yes ☐ No

TO: INTERNAL REVENUE SERVICE CENTER   Jan. 25, 1977
AUSTIN, TEXAS 78740

Dear Sirs:

This is the attached sheet containing 19a of Schedule C (Business Expenses)

```
19 a) Advertizing, TV, Radio, Newspapers            $13,239.32
   b) Answering service                                 264.00
   c) Banking                                           127.27
   d) Car(½) for business runs                          153.00
   e) Film Laboratory(printing, developing 35 mm film 3,359.70
   f) Freight                                         1,028.69
   g) Interest Loans                                    171.26
   h) Legal fees                                      1,000.00
   i) Miscellaneous                                     437.63
   j) Postage & box Rent                                 52.82
   k) Film screenings                                   217.00
   l) Location shooting, camera equipment, sound      4,731.93
   m) Telephone                                         725.56
   n) Theater Rental( 7 theaters)(1 week)            22,800.00
   o) Air travel & Hotels                             3,742.47
   p) Xerox                                              22.96
                                                   $ 54,074.40
                                                     54,073.61
```

Sincerely,

Palmer L. Rockey
Palmer Rockey

Feb. 7, 1977

Dear MaryAnn:

I sent your badge up by messenger. Since you say you need $1.50, I sent-on an extra 2 dollars in another letter to you, in accordance per verbal and written agreement between us.

I talked to the Sanger-Harris credit people. This is what to do. Fill out an application; tell them you have a job and are working; give them the address where you lived a long time here, tell them you've had an account over 4 years with Palmer Rockey, and that it has a number 1 credit rating. They will check it out, and on finding, that I've kept an excellent payment record, they will open an account under your name.

It's not how much money you make, I was told, but how you've made your payments over a long length of time. Since I've been Christianly honest in handling money, you have a fine chance for your own credit card.

Be grateful. When only one of the lepers came back after being healed, Josh didn't like it at all. And I'd hate to be where the other 9 are now.

I've delivered the junk mail as you requested.

In case I'm not in when you call, I've done what you've asked for per written agreement. I've set up a special lot for you at Bekins. You will find the Bekins papers in my PO Box. All your things are sealed up in boxes, and all you have to do is call, and they will deliver it to you for about $25.

I saved you a lot of money by making several trips to put all your belongings there. When you ask for them, they have assured me, that you can charge and pay back on a monthly basis. Your monthly storage bill is a cheap $4.80.

As you requested, all this was done by Feb. 1, 1976, per contract, and I request that you do things just as faithfully. I've also been working on the other things per verbal and written agreement. The man who acted arrogant and cut me off on the phone at the First Natl. in Dallas, has been removed. So has the man in California who didn't keep his word with me. I read in Variety that he no longer has his job.

"When you do it to one of these the least of my friends, you do it to me." Josh picks the right time and moment, then makes his powerful moves on behalf of his friends. "The wrongdoer pays for his wrongdoing, for there is no partiality." Thank God for that.

I will put your box key in this envelope in my box. PUT MY BOX KEY IN THE ENVELOPE AND LEAVE IT IN MY BOX. Send the checks, per agreement, for Feb. 18, and Mar. 4, 1977 to my box, since you now requested the badge back for work. Don't forget to endorse the checks.

For your own mental progress, besides what you say you are making(I'm glad to hear it)recall that when you called me to pick you up at the Lynn Restaurant(Metro), recall that your eyes were blank and faded, your complex completely white, your strength dangerously low. I firmly know that at the Maddly Towers you would've been unconscious and perhaps dead within 7 hours. When you came here, you slept for 2 whole days straight, ate excellent steaks and recouperated. That is at least 3 times in your life, wherein you were saved by me from deadly consequences. I hope you've progressed enough to realize it wasn't your psychiatrist who stopped by and picked you up when you were so low. For your own sake and future, remember kindly those who work closely with Josh.

I didn't open your mother's letter out of nosiness. I had not bee given any instructions about your leaving date or what to do wit personal mail because of your condition. So I had to open it to see if there was something of an emergency nature to relate to yo But I would recommend when you write or see her again, to include a Christian apology to her. It would help your mind and conscienc a lot. Remember a mother understands certain things a lot more graciously than others, as long as you level with her.

You'll probably be back working and out in a couple weeks, since I've been informed you've got only 50 days on your hospital insur

The other big batch of letters are at Bekins with the rest of you belongings, so nothing has been taken from you according to Josh' laws of justice. Forks, spoons, dishes, clothes, blankets, frying pans, sewing machine, dryers, gold set, you name them, they're all

You should have $126.00 in your credit union account. And soon yo should be receiving the other $350.00 from Blue Shield. I didn't use your checks you left me to withdraw money from your account.

"Man shall not live by bread alone, but by every word of God". An has come up that we'll have to discuss and come to an agreement later.

I intend to do all things according to Josh's justice, knowing fu well his command: "Seek first the kingdom of God and his justice and all these things will be added as well."

And what is the kingdom of God? "The kingdom of God is not just food and drink, but righteousness, peace and joy in the Holy Spi

I hope you find them again, the only way anyone can find them: L

to God's own words : "This is my Son in whom I am well pleased. Obey Him." I made my commitment many years ago, and I shall neve

break it, or his laws, knowingly or deceitfully. If there's anything I can do to help, leave word at 821-5647.

                                              Sincerely in Christ,

                                              Palmer

You can use my name for reference; also remember the woman you k Mechle, and other people at your work.

Form No. 380-DR—Subpoena—Civil

THE STATE OF TEXAS

No77-2436-DR/4

TO ANY SHERIFF OR ANY CONSTABLE OF THE STATE OF TEXAS—GREETING:
YOU ARE HEREBY COMMANDED to Subpoena

MARY A. ROCKEY TENDER $1.00
UNITED STATES POST OFFICE
TERMINAL ANNEX
207 S. Houston Street
Dallas, TX 75202

to appear before the DOMESTIC RELATIONS COURT #4 of Dallas County, Texas, on THURSDAY MAY 8 26, 19 77 at 1:30 o'clock P. M. then and there to give evidence for the RESPONDENT in a cause therein pending, in which MARY ANN ROCKEY, PETITIONER XXXXXX
and PALMER LOUIS ROCKEY, RESPONDENT XXXXXXX
and there remain from day to day and term to term, until discharged by the Court.

HEREIN FAIL NOT, but have you then and there this Writ, showing how you have executed the same.

WITNESS: Clerk of the District Courts of Dallas County, at office in the City of Dallas, this 20th day of May A.D., 19 77.

ATTEST: BILL SHAW
Clerk District Courts, Dallas County

By .... Deputy
Cathy Orr

DOMESTIC RELATIONS COURT #4
of Dallas County, Texas

IN THE MATTER OF THE MARRIAGE
OF MARY ANN ROCKEY AND

SUBPOENA
vs. CIVIL

PALMER LOUIS ROCKEY
ISSUED

This 20th day of May A.D. 19 77

BILL SHAW
Clerk District Courts

By: Cathy Orr .... Deputy

PALMER LOUIS ROCKEY, X PRO SE
5405 Gaston Ave., #201
Dallas, TX 75214
821-5647

THIS PROCESS WAS SERVED UPON YOU
AT 8:35 O'CLOCK P M
May 23 19 77
CONSTABLE PRECT. 6
DALLAS COUNTY, TEXAS
By .... Deputy

J. E. ......, Precinct .....
Constable, Dallas County, Texas

Texas Divorce Index, 1968-2002 Record

Name:	**Palmer L Rockey**
Estimated Birth Year:	abt 1922
Age:	55
Spouse's Name:	Mary A [Rockey]
Spouse's Estimated Birth Year:	abt 1947
Spouse's Age:	30
Divorce Date:	20 Jun 1977
Marriage Date:	2 Jun 1968
Number of Children:	0
County:	Dallas

Source Information:
Ancestry.com. *Texas Divorce Index, 1968-2002* [database online]. Provo, Utah: MyFamily.com, Inc., 2005. Original data: Texas Department of State Health Services. *Texas Divorce Index, 1968-2002*. Texas Department of State Health Services, Texas.

STATE OF CALIFORNIA
DEPARTMENT OF HEALTH SERVICES

CERTIFICATE OF DEATH

1. Name of Decedent - First	PALMER
2. Middle	—
3. Last	ROCKEY
4. Date of Birth	11/17/1921
5. Age	74
7. Sex	M
8. Date of Death	04/24/1996
9. Hour	0335
12. Marital Status	NVR. MRD.
13. Education	UNK
14. Race	CAUC
17. Occupation	UNK
20. Residence	2352 WESTWOOD BLVD
21. City	LOS ANGELES
22. County	LOS ANGELES
23. ZIP	90064
25. State	CALIFORNIA
Informant	COUNTRY VILLA NORTH CONV. HOSP., 3233 W. PICO BLVD., L.A. CA 90029
31. Father	UNK
33. Last	UNK
34. Birth State	UNK
35. Mother	UNK
37. Last	UNK
38. Birth State	UNK
39. Date of Disposition	05/09/1996
40. Place	L.A. CO CREM/CEM., L.A., CA
41. Type of Disposition	CR/BU
Embalmer	NOT EMBALMED
License No.	NONE
Funeral Establishment	LAC USC MED. CEN. MORT.
Signature Date	05/06/1996
101. Place of Death	COUNTRY VILLA N. CONV. HOSP.
Address	3233 W. PICO BLVD.
103. County	LOS ANGELES
104.	LOS ANGELES
107. Immediate Cause (A)	CARDIORESPIRATORY ARREST — MINS
Due to (B)	METASTATIC BRAIN DISEASE — 2 MOS
Due to (C)	RENAL CELL CARCINOMA — 6 MOS
112. Other Significant Conditions	CACHEXIA, GENERALIZED WEAKNESS, LEFT HEMIPLEGIA, ORGANIC BRAIN SYNDROME
Biopsy	NO
114. Physician Attended From	11/01/1995
Last Seen	04/23/1996
Physician	ARET AKIAN, MD, 5000 [redacted], L.A., CA 90027
Date Signed	05/02/1996

State Registrar: 4 X 2 0 0

001133817

This is to certify that this document is a true copy of the official record filed with the Office of Vital Records.

MICHAEL L. RODRIAN
STATE REGISTRAR OF VITAL RECORDS

DATE ISSUED: 01 MAY 23 PM 5:39

U.S. Veterans Cemeteries, ca.1800-2004 Record

Name:	**Palmer Rockey**
Veteran's Rank:	PVT AIR CORPS
Branch:	US Army
Last known address:	22495 Van Buren Boulevard Riverside, CA 92518
Birth Date:	17 Nov 1921
Death Date:	24 Apr 1996
Veteran Service Start Date:	16 May 1945
Veteran Service End Date:	7 Nov 1946
Interment Date:	28 May 1996
Cemetery:	Riverside National Cemetery
Buried At:	Section 47 Site 3535
Cemetery URL:	

Source Information:
National Cemetery Administration. *U.S. Veterans Cemeteries, ca.1800-2004* [database online]. Provo, Utah: MyFamily.com, Inc., 2005. Original data: National Cemetery Administration. *Nationwide Gravesite Locator*.

Copyright © 1998-2006. MyFamily.com Inc.

Chapter 8

A NEW CHAPTER IN LIFE

Palm gave up in 1973, and decided to make one of his other scripts into a movie. We named it "It Happened One Weekend". We borrowed from the Credit Union several times ($10,000 altogether, over a period of 4 years.).

We had to go before the Board of Directors several times and they were impressed with his knowledge of the business. They loaned us the money each time.

Every time we got $1000 ahead he would use it to shoot more scenes. The $1000 came from me working overtime every night.

We starred in the film together. He was the director. I was the script person—never having done it before. I had to help coordinate the whole thing. I had watched the filming in LA and learned how to do it.

His friend, Ron DiSalvo, who he flew in from California, had most of the talking parts along with Palm. We set Ron up in a hotel. Ron got mad and had an argument with Palm about his yelling at everybody. Palm explained to me, later, that you get more done being mean. While filming he acted mean and always in a hurry. I learned much of how to never shoot a film.

*   *   *

When "It Happened One Weekend" premiered at Canyon Creek Cinema, I rode in a limo to and from the Premier. It was announced on the radio and in the paper. I have some pictures of it. (The picture on the front of his album for "Scarlet Love" was taken at the Premiere of "It Happened One Weekend" by me.) The movie made very little money. Palm got sick that weekend it played and couldn't go back to check on attendance. The name was changed to "It Happened On Sunday" when it played in Denver and El Paso. It made more money than the Canyon Creek Premier, but never covered his expenses to make the film or distribute it.

When Palm couldn't find any suckers to distribute his picture he called Tom Laughlin to distribute it. Tom was in the process of distributing another "Billy Jack" film. Tom ran a background check on Palm because Tom told him that he needed to go to work and that I was supporting him. Palm was really angry about the flippant way Tom treated him. I presume Tom was not doing well himself in the business with his new sequel.

The Rock

Palm promulgated paranoia. At the end of our marriage he made me swear that I would support him until the movie made it. I wore the same dress and blouses for 7 years so he wouldn't have to buy me clothes. Finally I told Palm I needed new clothes. He bought me some pants and tops to match. I wore the same old brown coat for 10 years and a postal sweater that was almost worn out; always thinking I was working for Jesus. I always wore my hair long and pulled back at the nape of the neck and only wore eyebrow pencil for makeup. I walked downtown Dallas a lot for exercise and something to do. There were lots of prostitutes down there and Hari Krishna. HL Green's was the only store I could afford. It was a general merchandise store like Woolworth's.

Palm got a credit card at Sanger-Harris and started buying china and silverware. I still have half of it. We were not to put up Christmas decorations or celebrate any other Holiday. No Birthday presents were ever exchanged ("until we make it big", he said). He used to bring me back a piece of jewelry every time he flew somewhere to look for money, but that stopped in 1971. The last time he came back from a trip, just before I went into the hospital, all his jackets were filthy; like he had been sleeping on the streets in LA.

Then one day in 1976, the February before I left Palm, he told me something that completely changed my concept of him. When I got home from work at 4am that morning,

Palm told me that my father had died in a crash. Then Palm told me the clincher—the call had come several weeks ago and so the funeral was over and there was no sense in calling back. (Then Palm had the gall, in a letter written after I left him, to say that I should have called them back. What a hypocrite!)

Palm worked for a three weeks at the Parcel Post Annex at the Post Office because he wanted some more money for some scenes he needed for his film. Palm never wanted anyone to know he knew me at work. He denied it when asked by supervisors who knew the names of the day laborers. He didn't want anyone to know he was doing manual labor because he was a Producer, Director, Writer and Star of his film. He worked 3 weeks.

Chapter 9

MY LIFE

It was autumn again. The leaves were dying and so was my will to go on. I had to get a second job because they cut out overtime and Palm had some plans for that money. He couldn't get a fulltime job because of his position—"Producer, Director, Writer and Star". If anyone ever found out they would laugh at him. I got a job going from door to door with a directory for firemen, etc. done by The RL Polk Co. I did so well they wanted me to work full time in the office. They never knew I had a second job. I had lots of vacation and sick leave accumulated. Every time he left town for something, I took off on vacation pay for however many days he was gone. I went places on the bus, saw sights and went to a book store.

    I was never given any allowance. I always had 1 or 2 dollars in my billfold, except when I had to take a cab home, then, I was given more money. When I began to see that his movie was going nowhere but putting me in debt more and more I decided to study the bank statement. I studied it and found that they were taking $25 more out of my check than the payment on my loan, and it had accrued. It must have gone unnoticed by Palm as he would have had enough to spend on making another scene for his movie. $500 had accrued and I opened a checking account at the Credit Union and got a P.O. Box where I worked. Unfortunately for me it was right next to his. They kept putting my mail in his box. Thank heavens he just thought the company sending the advertising mail put the wrong address on the mail. He knew nothing about the checking account or that I had put the $500 in it. I spent some of it on books and sent for things through the mail to my P. O. Box.

Then, another strange thing happened. He told me about a situation that happened when I was at work the day before. The reason he told me was that he was afraid I would find out from SOMEONE ELSE. He explained that he had been going to a local supermarket and practicing singing his songs in his vehicle every day, parked in the parking lot. (I slept until late morning, after getting off work at 3:30 AM. He could have practiced after I left for work at 2 PM.) Yesterday, someone robbed the supermarket and a witness gave the police his license plate number after seeing someone suspicious, like they were casing the joint every day. How did the police react, with a squad of police, with rifles pointed at the door to our apartment? He looked out and quickly answered the door when they rang the bell. They searched the apartment and him. I guess he was able to talk them out of arresting him. I never heard from them, but he was sure afraid I would.

I don't know what sparked it but I think he insisted on me telling him my opinion of his movie. I tried to be diplomatic about it and told him it was disjointed and didn't make sense.

After I criticized his movie, which he treated as his child, he would not speak to me for 6 months. He made me cook my own meals. (He had been doing it previously.) I did nothing but eat, sleep and work for 3 years. And he stayed away when I was awake. We only were together when he picked me up at work at 3:30am, after I had worked 12 hours. He went to bed at 7pm so I could have the bed to myself. Every time we got any money ahead he spent it on something for his movie and no one dare criticize it or he would go into a tirade.

He kept telling me we would make tons of money soon. That worked for 8 years, but when I finally wised up, I was $10,000 in debt, which was one year's salary, and had a nervous breakdown.

Chapter 10

BREAKDOWN AND SEPARATION

I felt I was having a nervous breakdown and, instead of waiting for it to get worse, I decided to do something about it. Well, I went to put the wash in the machines in the apartment house and then went out the front door of the apartment house (no purse) just my wallet. I caught the bus and got off at Baylor Hospital, which wasn't that far from the apartment. I was admitting myself to the hospital psychiatric ward, hoping to get away from my husband and his controlling ways, his spending and my working too many hours. I went to admitting. The woman at the desk told me that a Doctor would have to admit me. It was a Friday and I called my regular Doctor, who called me back on one of the pay phones at the hospital. I told her my story and she said she knew a woman psychiatrist who would admit me. She called the psychiatrist and called me back. The Psychiatrist couldn't see me until Monday. I should check into a Motel and wait. I checked into the

The Rock

rundown Metro Motel across the street from Baylor. She prescribed a tranquilizer that hyped me up, so Saturday she tried another. It helped a little. It was the longest 2 days in my life. My family doctor said she thought Palm was a Manic Depressive, just from reading the interview with him, when "It Happened One Weekend" came out.

I had no cash, but one credit card and had gotten a checkbook from the Credit Union when I found the money. I walked to the nearest grocery store and bought snacks, sandwich fixing's. I ate one meal in the restaurant each day.

I finally had my meeting with the psychiatrist and she said that before she could treat me I would have to come up with $300. I had about $350 in checking.

She did tell me I needed a divorce and set up an appointment with a lawyer to file for divorce. She put me in the hospital immediately. I needed clothes etc. so I had to call my husband. Palm had called the police, but they wouldn't look for me. He came down to the Motel and I think he brought me the items I needed. Then he tried to convince me to come home. I went on to the hospital the day before Thanksgiving, instead.

I had to be out of the hospital on New Year's Day for the insurance to pay and I had my credit card to rent a room in the Baylor Tower. That was on a Monday.

I called Palm and he convinced me to come home, when he came down to the hotel to bring me clothes. When Wednesday came, the day I was to be put back in the hospital, his car broke down and since I had to be admitted that day, we had to carry my suitcases down Gaston Avenue, one mile to the hospital. Palm acted like he cared about me and made a scene and kissed me. He said all kinds of nice things before he left.

Palm still had me under his control, because he got a letter to me by an aide. He needed a letter authorizing him to pick up my check, so he could live on it. At some point during my stay I realized I would need to have some money to start over; that meant cutting him off from my paychecks. I kept the next one he sent up by one of the aides to have me sign. Then I told the Doctor that the fire-works were about to begin.

I don't know at what point I came to the realization that he spent his whole life living off women so he would not have to work. It was a shock to me to realize I had been duped for 8 1/2 years. It was like being in a cult. One time I had an original thought about the bible and he got mad and said, "I didn't tell you that!" I believed I was doing God's work—making it possible for him to get people to invest in making the life of Christ, The Prince of Peace. It reminds me of a cult person's mind. You believe in that person's goodness so much that you feel betrayed when you learn the truth.

I was in the hospital for another 1 ½ months—quite an experience. Entering the unit was even a scary experience, the first time. You could only get there by elevator. When the door opened you were ushered into a glass enclosed area. You were accompanied by an aide. You had to state your name into an intercom. There were 3 or 4 women at desks, behind a glass enclosure, checking people in or out.

One night when I was near the desk, 3 burly policemen came in bringing a 5' 3" small woman. All of a sudden this girl became a wild cat trying to get away from confinement. She climbed the glass around the desks and ran and ran on the glass. It took three burly men to subdue her. The screams were horrifying and the noise frightening. They finally gave her a shot of something to calm her. It was quite a sight.

Being in Baylor was a really scary experience. All phases of the mentally ill were thrown together in one day room. The sane ones hung out together on one end of the room and talked with each other about their problems. The others wandered around saying scary things and doing scary things.

We had Art Therapy in the morning and several Group meetings to talk about our problems. I saw my doctor every day at her office during the work week, but not on the weekend.

As soon as I got there they began experimenting with different drugs to see what would help me. One time, they gave me an anti-psychotic drug on a Friday. It made it impossible for me to speak. They called the doctor. She had left for the weekend and could not be reached. I couldn't talk for three days. They kept giving me the drug because they couldn't stop it until the doctor said to. On Monday, when I saw Dr Marilyn, I couldn't tell her anything. I had to write it down for her. She changed the medicine.

Several times, frightening things happened:

I was sitting on a couch with some depressed people, talking. A young man ran over and began yelling and screaming some crazy stuff at us. This man had been perfectly calm the minute before. One of the aides came over and led him away. We all sat in shocked silence.

One day, I noticed an elderly lady sitting at a table by herself, holding a heated conversation with an invisible person. I thought I would help and went over and sat beside her. I asked her a question and she turned suddenly and said angrily, "Can't you see I'm having a conversation with Ruby? Don't interrupt me!"

Another woman vomited involuntarily and sprayed it everywhere. Even on people around her. The cleaning people tried to get it out of the carpet, but couldn't. It was disgusting. She had to be sent to Terrell (the area mental hospital) to recover, we were told, and I could see that half the people were not far behind her.

There were lots of people who had tried to commit suicide or, who wanted to. One man had shot himself in the head and survived—he looked awful! (When he got out, he attempted it again by shooting himself in the head.

I know this because I was hospitalized a year later and he was back. He had lost his eyesight this time.)

One woman had horrific dreams when she slept and you could hear her yelling at night. The strange thing, though, was that she only became this way when she became pregnant and it stopped after the baby was born. No one thought the baby would come to term, but it did.

At that time, I had not heard of Bulemia, etc., but I was introduced to someone who had it, at the hospital. The woman involved ate only orange juice and crackers. She finally admitted, to our small group, that she had an eating disorder. She took two showers every day and was skinny as a rail, but folded her dress around her waist to make herself look bigger. Her cheeks were sunk in and all her bones were showing.

There was one young man, who was rich, but crazy like a fox. His family kept putting him into the mental hospital to straighten his mind out. He sat all day and watched the doors that exited the unit. One day he disappeared. He had figured out how to escape. Later I heard that he sued his family to leave him alone and won his freedom from them. One more crazy man on the streets!

The teenagers were on another floor, but periodically, when not attending school, they were allowed to mingle with the adults. Many had run away from home and were incarcerated for 3 or 4 months. When a teenager became out of control, he or she was tied to a chair in the middle of the gathering room and made to sit there for hours or days, depending on what they had done. An aide had to sit in front of them the whole time. It was like watching a tied animal, as they would fight back.

We wore our street clothes and not bed clothes. When first admitted, we were not permitted calls or able to go outside for two weeks. They fed us cafeteria style in the gathering room.

We had several lockdowns, when the nurses would look for contraband. They looked through all your stuff in your room, removed switch covers and looked in the light fixtures.

I was very quiet and just watched and watched the situations evolving around me. It was like a bad dream.

I had a roommate who was coming down off drugs and she slept very little. She was in the bathroom most of the night. She was a good roommate. Others were not. The next roommate plucked her eyelashes out and would have sex with strangers, when she could. She was married and a teacher. We went walking one time and she was walking crazy like. She explained that she had to pick up the bobby pins on the ground as she walked. I never went walking with her again! Another roommate had a problem because she felt like having sex all the time. Her husband couldn't stay home from work to satisfy her. One roommate wanted to commit suicide. She was really depressed and felt no way out of her problems. I couldn't help her!

Two months later, when I had rented an apartment, near the hospital, I came back to pick up my things, where Palm and I had lived. Upon entering, I pulled the lock on the inside of the door over so he couldn't get in with the key. Unfortunately, he came back while I was there and when he knew I was in there, he went crazy and started kicking the door down. I didn't want the police called, so I opened the door. He told me he ought to beat me like his uncle did his wife. Palm had me against the wall and his fist ready to strike me. He hit the wall instead and let me go. I left scared, but in one piece.

I moved into the apartment after getting out of the hospital. I lived the next block down from the Barnett Tower, at Baylor Hospital on Junius Street.

There is a parking garage there now.

I saw Dr Marilyn every day in her office and then when the insurance wouldn't pay I had to borrow almost $800 to pay her off. From then on she stayed within the insurance company's limits and only collected what they would pay.

Palm was "uniquely crazy" as his divorce lawyer (Mr Raggio, of Raggio and Raggio Law Firm) described him to my Doctor. That was after Mr Raggio learned Palm had no money, but mine. Palm was dropped as Mr. Raggio's client. He became his own lawyer after that.

Then I got a dreaded call. His precious car had been stolen—his beat up '54 Chevy. He just 'knew' I had done it. He had been in several accidents that were not his fault and collected on the other people's insurance, as he had no insurance. Palm never fixed the car so it was a mess with both doors beat in and the back end bunged up. The police finally found it abandoned somewhere close, out of gas.

During the time I was working, I met him on the bus, as he knew my schedule. It was really scary as he harassed me, by walking up close and threatening me.

Palm even tried to harass me in the hallway at the courthouse when my lawyer left my side to talk to another lawyer. I walked away toward my lawyer, agitated. My lawyer looked up and saw me coming. He asked me what was wrong. Palm didn't bother me as long as my lawyer was near after that.

When we went before the judge, the judge ordered our accounts frozen at the bank. Next thing I knew my lawyer called to tell me I had to see the judge again, in chambers, because my husband had sweet talked a teller into giving him $2000 of the $4000 from our IRS return that had been deposited to our joint account. I was scared to death because I knew Palm would argue and argue. He did! The judge asked him 40 times, if once, "Did you take the money from the account, Yes or No!" He would not admit it until the judge said, "You either answer now, or go to jail." Palm said, "Yes." That took an hour of questioning!! The judge told him he didn't want to hear any more arguments as to why he took it. It has to be returned by a certain date or you go to jail. "Bring your toothbrush, on that date, if you don't have the money." the Judge said. He gave him about a month to get it.

I didn't have to be there on that date, as I was in Nevada with my family that June. I called from there to see if he had to go to jail. My lawyer said that Palm approached him in the Courthouse bathroom, joyously explaining that he had the money, but not telling him how he got it. He had used $2000 to pay bills, thinking that half of the IRS return was his after he put the full amount in our joint account.

At the final hearing, he received none of the money, but wanted to tell me how to spend the money. That was nixed by the judge. The judge told him to get a job, just like the judge had a job and came to work each day. He asked him about his doctorate and Palm said he would have to study to keep it up, but he was a Producer, Director and Writer. The judge asked him if he received any pay for that and Palm said, "No." That's when he told him to get a job, again.

Palm had brought a letter from a Doctor that said he had had a heart attack and couldn't work. That didn't cut any ice with the judge. He told him if he could come down to the court he could work at something.

My lawyer had to listen to him for hours (for which I paid) about crazy stuff. His asset paper listed each knife, fork and spoon and all personal belongings in-between, as we had no assets, just horrendous debts. I ended up with the $10,000 debt to pay the Credit Union by payroll deduction. He ended up with the rest of the Credit cards and bank loans. But the movie was his scot-free. Because if I touched it, I would owe all the money the investors put into it. I had no idea how much that was.

It took 7 months to get my divorce finalized and $2000.

Chapter 11

A NEW BEGINNING

My psychiatrist saw me every day, it seemed. She did nothing but listened and offered no comments. She was very nervous and opened her cabinet beside her chair many times during each visit, first to look at her teeth in a full grimace. Then she would put that mirror away and start rubbing her eyes (she did lots of that) but would never look at me. It was like I wasn't there. Then she would open the cabinet again and study the 10 or 12 bottles of medicine and take a pill from one. Back to checking her eyes with the mirror to see if there were any loose eye lashes. Then she would think of someone to call, mostly home about her baby, and she would actually excuse herself. After I talked on for 45 minutes, it was time to go. I always cried, which should have told her something was wrong. I was in Group therapy, with no one who had what I had, so I didn't really receive any help with my problems. It was always someone else's problems we dealt with.

I worked in an office after I went back to work, instead of working on the machines. Then I learned to interact with others. Several years went by and one day I came into the office I was working in, where a friend was reading the newspaper. I sat down in my chair, which was next to her chair, and began to work. All of a sudden she started laughing at what she saw on one page and threw the paper down in front of me. The shock was instant and I gasped at the picture of Palm and another girl in a full page ad for "Scarlet Love" playing at Northpark I Theater. The office was in an uproar after that, as they knew about my ex-husband making a picture, but never expected it to be shown. Then curiosity set in. Did he cut me out of it? What is it like now? So we decided that some of us would go see it.

According to the newspaper interview of Palmer, he talked people into putting up money for distributing the film in theaters. It showed at Northpark I—the best theater in town, for three weeks. That was March of 1980.

Palm went by PL Rockey in the ad in the paper in Dallas. The girl who was walking with him was taller than him, blonde, and was a model from the Kim Dawson Agency. She wore a tam like I did in the movie, but not like I wore it, at a saucy angle. I have the interviews from the newspapers. He even made a record of his own compositions and sang the songs in the movie—"Scarlet Love".

When we got to the theater, we were early, so one friend, Buzz, and I sat in a restaurant waiting for the other friend,

AJ, to arrive. We could see the theater entrance from the window of the restaurant. When we saw AJ, we got up and started walking toward the theater where AJ went in. When we were about 100 feet from the door, Palm came out in a hurry, like he'd seen a ghost. He turned and looked at us and increased his walking speed to a run. AJ was laughing when we came in and told us he shook hands with Palmer and told him his ex-wife was coming to see the film. Palm denied ever having been married. We were the only ones in the theater and talked out loud, laughing during the whole showing. Some people left after it started and got their money back.

Palm hadn't cut me out of the film. His film became really disjointed when I divorced him, as he had to substitute my part, which was the lead female role in the film.

The film began with about 10 girls in bikinis holding hands in a circle and walking first one way and then another. It was really bad with extra crazy scenes in it. He had done all the work of mixing the sound and picture together. Palmer had the sound man record all sorts of sounds to add to scenes in his film, so he wouldn't have to rent the sounds in a studio.

He ruined the film with the loud music, trying to appeal to the young crowd. His singing made the picture unbearable to listen to. His songs were very depressing with no emotion. The way he put the film together made no sense. The original script that I read was good. It was supposed to be a thriller, with gore in it.

Palm left town soon afterwards. He went to LA. I found that out from the Post Office. He had a P.O. Box in L.A. until 1998, even though he died in 1996. The reason I believe the P.O. Box was still open in his name after his death was because, I believe a woman lived with him and probably got mail in that box until 1998, when she moved on. On one background check she was at the same address as he was until 1998.

Chapter 12

THE FINAL DAYS

I started looking up Palmer Rockey when I retired from the Post Office after 35 years. I had more time to work on the computer. That was in 2000. I wanted to find out where he was, but found out, after a free trial period on Ancestry.com, that he was dead. I did a search on the Social Security Death Index and found that he had died in 1996 in Los Angeles. My husband hated him, so I had to search Palm's name when my second husband wasn't around. I probed further on all places on the website when I joined Ancestry for a year, to do Genealogical family research.

    I found Palm's and my marriage and divorce info, his WW II enlistment info, Census info and his Social Security application form. I got bold after that and asked King County for his birth certificate and got it. I got more bold and asked California for his death certificate and got it. I have been through every mention of him on the Internet and know now that I am the only one who knows the true and full story about Palmer Rockey.

That has led me to write down my life with Palmer Rockey and then his earlier life and what I know of his life after our divorce.

Chapter 13

THE REAL PALMER ROCKEY

Let's begin at the beginning:

Both of Palmer's parents came over from Italy in 1907 according to documents in my possession. They may have been on the same ship.

Joseph Rockey (Rocchi), Palmer's father, was born in Naples Italy.

On the 1920 Census, Joseph Rocchi was incarcerated in a mental hospital in Napa California. The next time you find him, is in 1921 in Seattle Washington as the father of Palmer, who lost his wife, Jessie (Palmeria) Mironte-Merante, at childbirth. Joseph used the spelling of Rocky on the death certificate for Jesse, but Rockey on the birth certificate for Palmer. Joseph more than likely changed his name to avoid re-incarceration or to avoid detection as having a record of incarceration in a mental institution. Palmer's name on his birth certificate is Palmiero Rockey, with no middle name. He was named after his mother, whose name was Palmeria, but her nickname was Jessie.

Palmer was born in Swedish Hospital in Seattle Washington at 9:30 AM on 11-17-1921 with CL Templeton, MD delivering him. His mother, Jessie, had eclampsia and died 2 hours later at 11:30 AM. She must have been rushed to the hospital when she had a convulsion, as that is the first bad sign something is wrong. Otherwise, Palmer may have been born at home with a midwife assisting his mother, as most people of lower means were born at home back then. The only record of birth at that time was mostly from Baptismal records.

Jessie must have married Joseph Rockey, because, at 25, she was considered an old maid. Joseph may have been a renter, as about 6 men of various last names were listed in the house with the Merante's on the 1920 Census.

You next find Joseph Rockey in Newcastle Washington, a coal mining town, northeast of Seattle WA. He was working for the Pacific Coach Coal Co, as a fireman, when he filled out a form for the military. He was of medium build, with brown eyes and dark hair, born on May 9, 1896.

At some point he went to chicken farming and in the 1930 Census, Palmer (9) was with him. He gave his name as Joey on the Census, but it looks like Joy. Shortly, thereafter, Palmer was removed from Joseph's custody for child abuse—placing Palmer, butt first on a hot coal stove top. The Merante's came up to Newcastle and surreptitiously checked on Palmer's condition. They waited in their car outside of the chicken farm driveway to talk with Palmer, he told me. Joseph was incarcerated in Steilacoom, the mental hospital at the time, after this incident.

He died there in 1939, at the age of 43, I believe, as Palmer was 18 and missed some school that year. It tore Palmer up, the death of his father, as he cried when he told me about his death. Joseph was young when he died.

Jessie's parents were Angelo and Marie Merante from Italy and they resided at the same location all their lives in Seattle Washington—Elmwood Ave. Angelo worked for the city surfacing streets in Seattle. When he retired, he had a nervous breakdown and was hospitalized, according to Palmer. Marie, his grandmother, died in 1966 at the age of 92, Palmer said.

Palmer had a good life with his grandparents, as his father's chicken ranch helped pay for his expenses and education at the Catholic Schools he attended.

Palmer played baseball or went to the theater to watch movies and dream of being a STAR. He never got in trouble as a kid or as a young man.

Palmer told me he had a chance at a baseball career until he injured his ankle in a bus accident. As far as I can find out, the bus accident never happened. But he missed quite a bit of time in his senior year of high School. I believe his father died that year and he suffered a nervous breakdown. Because he didn't play baseball his senior year of High

School, he had no chance to show off his talents to the baseball scouts.

Palm's description of the accident went thus: He was riding on a city bus, when the bus ran over a 2 x 4 in the road. It came through the floor of the bus and broke his ankle. "I never could play baseball again." Palm told me.

He pulled one lift out of his shoe and told me one leg was shorter than the other because of the accident. (Upon closer examination I found a lift in his other shoe also and it dawned on me that he had a complex about being short.)

Right after he graduated from Seattle Prep High School, he signed up for a Social Security card on 6-5-1940 at the age of 18. They asked for a middle name, so he gave himself the middle name of Louis and first put Rocchi, crossed it out and someone, other than him, printed Rockey (Probably because his Birth Certificate said Rockey.) He printed his name instead of signing his name, so it was crossed out and he signed the application.

Palmer's first job was with Boeing in Seattle, as his WW II Enlistment stated he was an airplane fabric and dope (glue) worker. He was single with no dependents. He enlisted on May 16, 1945 at Ft Lewis Washington as a Private.

After he got out in 1946, Palmer went into the Seminary at St Edwards College in Kenmore Washington to become a priest in the Catholic Church.

He lasted 3 years and when he came out he went to Seattle University for 1 year, graduating in 1950 with his

BA. (Seattle University was part of Seattle Prep when it was first started, but separated in 1933. Seattle College became a University in 1948.)

In 1950 Palmer entered Graduate School at St Louis University. At that time St Louis University had the top ranking Graduate School in Catholic Philosophy, which was Palmer's major. It was also run by the Jesuits, as his High School and Seattle University were. He received his MA in February, 1952. He wrote his thesis on "The Moral Philosophy of Giambattista Vico."

Palmer never could keep his birth year right as he put 1922, instead of 1921, on his "Vita Auctoris" (Latin for Author's Life) on his MA and Doctoral Theses. Both theses were on Giambattista Vico. Giam was from Naples, like Palm's father. I imagine this is why he chose Dr. Vico (1668-1744, a philosopher), for his theses.

In 1952, Palmer was appointed assistant in philosophy and was made an instructor in philosophy in 1954. He bought his 1954 Chevrolet to celebrate getting a job as instructor and had his picture taken when he got his PhD.

That is the younger picture you see on the Internet.

During the years from 1952 to 1956, Palmer translated 3 books; two by Luis Colomer from Spanish to English and one by Dr Pius Parsch from German to English. All of the books were about the Catholic Church and are being sold on the Internet from $8.18 to $35.99, plus postage.

As usual, Palmer was not satisfied with a PhD because you did not earn much money from teaching or being a Philosopher. He entered Medical School at St Louis University. He did well, but not like he expected in highest grades, so he made a decision to go to Hollywood, his biggest dream yet.

He began training at an acting school that hosted many of the famous stars.

He met Ron DiSalvo and they made a "B" movie in black and white. Nothing became of it, so, according to Palmer, he saved two rolls of film and put the rest in the landfill. His friend, Ron DiSalvo kept the two rolls for him until Palmer asked for one for "It Happened One Weekend". He asked Ron to play a part in the film and sent him an airline ticket. He put him up at a motel in Dallas. We rented a Station Wagon to pick up the coffin and Ron, also. (We used an extra coffin from a Funeral Home in Dallas. I hope it wasn't used for viewing!) We set it up on a stand in the Highland Park area on a little hill. I had to get in it for several scenes. How creepy!! But, I was told by Palmer that that was part of show business and I would do it if I wanted to be an actress.

I digress a minute: I met him in 1966 and we moved to Dallas in 1968.

We were baptized in the First Baptist Church of Dallas by W. A. Criswell, March 10, 1968. I married Palmer Rockey on June 2, 1968 in W.A. Criswell's study at the

First Baptist Church, with W.A. Criswell officiating. I was 21 and he was 46.

I have my baptismal records with my maiden name marked out and Mrs. Palmer Rockey put in its place. On 5-10-1972, we changed to another denomination by request. It was to get money from someone of another denomination.

Another momentous occasion in our lives was that he officially copyrighted "The Prince of Peace" that he had been working on so long and trying to raise money for. That was October 14, 1968.

By 1973, Palmer had given up making the life of Christ and began plans for his movie to be named by me: "It Happened One Weekend". We borrowed $10,000 from the Dallas Postal Credit Union on my name and with my Retirement put up for surety. Altogether we spent $12,795.66 on shooting the film according to IRS returns for that year. Then it played at Canyon Creek Cinema in October of 1974, making $696.25 but spending $19,034.00 for that year.

For 1975, he filed as a self employed filmmaker and spent $20,075.84 and made nothing on the film. That was just for shooting other scenes and running places trying to raise money to show it somewhere. The PO cut off the overtime I was working and he couldn't afford to shoot anything; so when an opportunity came for him to work some 19 days at the PO, he took it. I still have the paperwork from his employment from 9-19-75 to 10-7-75 for $5.63 an hour. It was for an emergency mail situation. The new machines for parcels would not work and the PO hired many people to handle the parcels, mostly relatives and friends of employees who knew about the situation.

By 1976, he was desperate to play the movie somewhere. Palmer played the movie in El Paso and Denver at some drive-ins that were still around at the time. He titled it "It Happened on Sunday" for those world premiers. We made $7860 in both places but spent $54,729.61; that was a net loss of $46,869.61. At that point, I decided to divorce him!!!!

He made me promise to help him until the film made him some money. Of course that was by coercion and my settlement on the divorce annulled that promise.

I filed for divorce and had the first of many hearings on February 22, 1977 to put a temporary Restraining Order against him and a Show Cause order.

One statement was "Do not make withdrawals from any checking or savings account."

My second filing was his list of assets, which consisted of 48 items of household use, nothing about what he owed. The 3rd filing was my inventory, consisting of 3 loans at the Credit union to the tune of $8360.56. Said loans were for Production of the 35mm Picture: "Scarlet Warning 666" as he renamed it, $40,000 in a Promissory Note to Rick Pew in 1976 for production and distribution of Scarlet Warning 666, and a loan at First National Bank for $1000. Deluxe

General of Hollywood for production of Scarlet Warning 666 to the tune of $10,300. He owed department stores: Sanger-Harris, Sears and Titches' minimal amounts.

The next filing was for Contempt of Court for cashing an IRS check and spending half of it to pay his bills. He forged my name to the check. He sweet talked a teller into allowing him to do this, as there was a Court Order that froze the account.

His answer came from Raggio and Raggio Law Firm as Palmer's lawyers.

Palmer told the court that he did not willfully disobey the court order, as he had told ME (but not the court) that he would give me half of the check and he would have the other half. He wrote down what bills he paid with his half. The judge didn't buy it, as it clearly stated neither one of us could cash the check. The judge would decide who got the check. Mr. Raggio dropped him after this loss.

May 2, 1977. Palmer was found in Contempt of Court and ordered to pay back the $2000 he spent, by May 26, 1977. Unless the money was in the account by June 2, 1977 (He was given an extension.) he would be jailed for 72 hours. He came up with the money, when he saw the judge wouldn't back down.

Our Property Settlement gave him sole ownership of the movie: "Scarlet Warning 666" aka "It Happened One Weekend" aka "It Happened On Sunday". But it doesn't say "Scarlet Love".

I got the check, as you probably guessed. He got the 1954 Chevrolet.

And all the debts, except the Credit Union loans.

This divorce took place on June 20, 1977, when he was 55 and I was 30.

In February 1980, Scarlet Love appeared on the scene, with PL Rockey plastered all over the papers in full page ads for the movie. I did a credit check on him and found some very interesting things. It showed 2 people at his address—a P.O. Box. He didn't give a street address. Palmer was robbing from Peter to pay Paul, as he had borrowed money from all the banks in Dallas. He also bought a car from General Motors with no income. I imagine he told General Motors his film was going to play at North Park, it was 2 months before the film came out. He had AB-Rock Productions since 1969 on the credit report (which was a lie, since ABBA Productions was on IRS returns during our marriage.).

Shortly after "Scarlet Love" played North Park Theater, Palmer departed the city for LA, California.

I remarried in August of 1980 and my husband and I were married 30 years.

On a background check, I found that Palmer gave as a residence at one point a Lutheran Church, then several different locations in LA. It appears he was living with a woman at one point, just before he went into the Nursing

Home. He had gotten a Security Guard license and worked 10 years to qualify for Social Security. He entered the Country Villa North Convalescent Hospital, 3233 W. Pico Blvd, LA CA 90029, on 11-1-95 and died on 4-24-96. He died of Cardiorespiratory arrest, caused by metastatic brain disease, due to Renal Cell (Kidney) Carcinoma Cancer. He was buried at Riverside National Cemetery, 22495 Van Buren Blvd, Riverside CA.

No one claimed his body; so many items were unknown on his Death Certificate. That is, also, why he was interred at Riverside on 5-28-96.

He had served in the military and was indigent at the time of death.

He had been in the Army Air Corp from 5-16-45 to 11-7-46 and went to school on the GI Bill.

At one time, Palmer was going to have a chain of restaurants that served only chicken, mainly in different sauces and served on rice. I found this recipe among the ones I saved, with his name on it.

ROCKEY'S CHICKEN

6 chicken breasts	¼ c melted butter
2 egg yolks	1 Tbl salt
1/2 c honey	1 tsp Paprika
¼ c Soy Sauce	½ tsp pepper
1/4 c lemon juice	

Beat egg yolks slightly. Blend in honey, Soy Sauce, lemon juice, butter, salt, paprika and pepper. Dip chicken in sauce and place in pan. Bake uncovered at 350 degrees for 1 hour, basting continuously.

Chapter 14

"SCARLET LOVE"— THE PLOT THICKENS

THE PLOT OF SCARLET LOVE: (aka. It Happened One Weekend, etc.)

The plot of "Scarlet Love": (aka. It Happened One Weekend, aka. It Happened On Sunday, aka. Scarlet Warning 666), was that the bad twin brother, Jack (played by Palm) was trying to kill his twin brother, Bruce (also played by Palm). It happened one weekend, on an estate somewhere in Texas. There were also twin sisters, who were the sisters of Bruce and Jack. (How convoluted!) One sister was Frances (played by Sherry Moore, she says in one article.); but I, Cookie Ann, played the roles in some places. I don't remember the name of the other sister. Frances dies and the other twin suffers a breakdown because of Frances' death.

The film was supposed to begin with the death of Frances, but Palm changed it to a scene of bikini clad young women in high-heeled boots holding hands and going around in a circle, first one way, then the other way. We shot that scene in a studio with a wood floor. The wood floor sounded out of place on a beach scene, as it was supposed to be on a beach on the estate. It was supposed to be part of the dark magic going on on the estate.

Palmer had the sound man, Bruce Shearin, record all sorts of sounds to add to scenes in his film, so he wouldn't have to rent the sounds in a studio when he edited the film.

As Bruce, Palm was continually running throughout the film, even in a parking garage. He pulled a ligament in his leg in one scene, where he was running uphill. His leg turned black with blood under the skin. He didn't go to the Doctor, as the "shooting must go on". I rubbed his leg hard to relieve the pain and that spread the blackness. It went away eventually over several months. He didn't try running very much after that. He was 52 years old at the time and out of shape. Palm walked a lot, but never ran to keep in shape. He was never overweight, though.

My character, Frances, appeared in a casket and then her twin appeared in a cemetery, confused and wandering around in a long skirted, black velvet suit with a black hat and a thick black veil over her face.

Frances and her sister wore very dark makeup to "hide who I really was" in real life, from people who knew me at the Post Office. That was ridiculous as well, as no one came to see the movie.

The Rock

Palmer had a good storyline, but kept adding scenes that had no impact on the storyline, but made it disjointed.

Several scenes were shot at a horse ranch in Plano. They involved watching a horse walk around on a moving horse walker and then, the same horse being spooked in a stall.

"Jaws" came out while we were filming and Palmer had to include something about "shark jaws" in the dialogue of one scene. Palmer, as Bruce or Jack, spoke most of the dialogue along with Ron DiSalvo, his friend from the "black and white" film. They were the most experienced actors.

Since love scenes were "in", Palm added one with an actress never before seen in the film.

Then Palm decided to shoot some scenes with a belly dancer. They were great scenes, but still had nothing to do with the plot.

In the winter of '73 or '74, an ice storm hit Dallas and the trees along the streets where we lived, made it look like a "Winter Wonderland." It was so beautiful, Palm wanted to film it, but couldn't get together a crew in time. That scene would have made no sense to the story, as the plot happened one SUMMER weekend.

Palmer incorporated his two black and white film scenes from his first "B" movie that he directed and starred in. The scenes were with Palm alone in one scene and the other he was arguing with Ron DiSalvo in a locker room.

The scene with Palm alone had him taking a white dove out of a cage while wearing white gloves. He did some hockus-pockus and put the dove back in the cage. (Again, there was no connection to anything in the film at hand.) Until, he thought of something.

Trying to make a connection in "Scarlet Love" to the black and white scenes, Palm bought two white doves, a male and female, that he named, Hanny and Manny. When we took them to Highland Park to film them, he let one out to walk on the ground. Of course, it flew into the nearest tree. I had to go home to get ready for work, so I missed the ensuing fun and games. The cameraman left and Palm had to climb the tree, get out on a limb and grab the bird. About two hours later, and to the many guffaws of those passing by, he grabbed the bird.

We gave the pair to the zoo after finishing with them, as they crapped everywhere, when they were out of the cage. We lived in an apartment, at the time, so that was a no-no.

I learned much from Palmer, especially how not to shoot a film. Palm ruined the film with the loud music, while trying to appeal to a younger crowd. His singing made the picture unbearable to listen to. His songs were very depressing and lifeless.

"Scarlet Love" became really disjointed when I divorced him, because he had to substitute someone else for Frances.

Palm tried to make out to investors that the film was of the "last days" during the "Tribulation." At least that was his spiel when I was with him.

It turned out to be a "tribulation" just to watch "Scarlet Love."

The film had no rhyme or reason in the end. The original script was a good story, but was ruined by Palmer trying to appeal to too many groups of people.

I don't believe Bruce ever found out why his brother, Jack, was trying to kill him or else if he did, it was lost on the audience, who were laughing at all the goof-ups in the filming.

I know that the three of us who endured the screening of "Scarlet Love", laughed so hard in parts, that we lost out on the dialogue that could have made the movie believable or at least understandable. As it was, the movie was action packed, with no reason to the actions of the people in the film.

It reminds me of Ed Wood's life, in the film by that name, starring Johnny Depp. He shot one-take scenes, even when nothing went right in the scene.

Palmer was proud of his one-take scenes. One scene in Palmer's film, where Bruce was trying to get away from Jack (Palmer as Bruce), pulled out really slowly from a parking place, putting on the brakes several times before he got out of the parking place. It was really a hoot!! Another time he had some over-stuffed beret hats on, and was playing with a dove. In one scene he wore a red beret, like a baker's hat, with a red shirt and in the other scene he wore a bright sky blue shirt and baker's beret. He looked so ridiculous that you had to laugh! After talking and laughing we missed the inane plot of the movie.

No wonder it never made the Oscars!!!

The End

SOME INTERESTING FACTS AND OBSERVATIONS FROM WIKIPEDIA

Newcastle, Washington's earliest coal mining area (1874-1963) is NE of Seattle. Because of that it was the Great Northern Railway's first link from Seattle. (This is where Joseph Rockey worked in 1930 with Palmer in tow.)

Naples (Napoli) (Neopolis was the first name, meaning "New City" in Greek). Naples is considered on the West Coast of Italy. It is known for its rich history, art, culture, architecture, music (opera) and food. It is one of the oldest cities (2,800 years old) in the world. Founded as a Greek colony in the 9th or 8th Century BC, it is by the Gulf of Naples (the second largest seaport in the world after Hong Kong.). (Could this be where Joseph Rocchi sailed from? Could the Merante family also, have been on the same ship?)

Naples is between two volcanic areas, Mt Vesuvius and the Phelegaean Fields. Pompeii, The Palace of Caserta and the Herculeum are various sites in the immediate vicinity of Naples.

Naples had a key role in the transmission of Greek culture to Roman society. It eventually became a Roman Republic and cultural center. Virgil received part of his education there. The inhabitants of Naples maintained the Greek language and customs. (Could this be the Italian dialect Palmer spoke at home?)

Between 1282 and 1816, it was ruled by the Kingdom of Naples and then in 1861 united with Sicily and became "The Two Sicilies" capital. (Could this be where Palmer got his education in conning people?)

Naples is known as the most densely populated major city in Italy and the fourth largest. It was the most bombed city in Italy in WWII. Pizza originated in Naples. It was first fried and then oven baked.

Hannibal was repulsed because of Naples strong walls. Claudius and Tiberius chose to holiday in Naples. (Palmer Rockey visited Naples on his Grand Tour of Italy.) Palmer's favorite philosopher, Giambattista Vico (1668-1744) was from Naples and so was Palmer's father, Joseph.

St Louis University is the oldest University west of the Mississippi. It was founded in 1818 by Reverend Louis Guillaume Valentin Dubourg. It is located on Lindell Blvd (Lindell's Grove). It became a Jesuit school in 1827.

Dubourg was Bishop of Louisiana and the Floridas.

Dubourg was born in Haiti and educated in France. Ordained in 1790, he fled France during the revolution in 1792 to exile in Spain. Spain went to war with France in 1793, so Dubourg fled on a ship to Baltimore where his brother had fled to earlier. He was appointed President of Georgetown College on October 1, 1796, serving to 1799. During this time he met George Washington.

Then Dubourg founded St Mary's College (a French College) and ran a lottery to support it. Then he went to

SOME INTERESTING FACTS AND OBSERVATIONS FROM WIKIPEDIA

Newcastle, Washington's earliest coal mining area (1874-1963) is NE of Seattle. Because of that it was the Great Northern Railway's first link from Seattle. (This is where Joseph Rockey worked in 1930 with Palmer in tow.)

Naples (Napoli) (Neopolis was the first name, meaning "New City" in Greek). Naples is considered on the West Coast of Italy. It is known for its rich history, art, culture, architecture, music (opera) and food. It is one of the oldest cities (2,800 years old) in the world. Founded as a Greek colony in the 9th or 8th Century BC, it is by the Gulf of Naples (the second largest seaport in the world after Hong Kong.). (Could this be where Joseph Rocchi sailed from? Could the Merante family also, have been on the same ship?)

Naples is between two volcanic areas, Mt Vesuvius and the Phelegaean Fields. Pompeii, The Palace of Caserta and the Herculeum are various sites in the immediate vicinity of Naples.

Naples had a key role in the transmission of Greek culture to Roman society. It eventually became a Roman Republic and cultural center. Virgil received part of his education there. The inhabitants of Naples maintained the Greek language and customs. (Could this be the Italian dialect Palmer spoke at home?)

Between 1282 and 1816, it was ruled by the Kingdom of Naples and then in 1861 united with Sicily and became "The Two Sicilies" capital. (Could this be where Palmer got his education in conning people?)

Naples is known as the most densely populated major city in Italy and the fourth largest. It was the most bombed city in Italy in WWII. Pizza originated in Naples. It was first fried and then oven baked.

Hannibal was repulsed because of Naples strong walls. Claudius and Tiberius chose to holiday in Naples. (Palmer Rockey visited Naples on his Grand Tour of Italy.) Palmer's favorite philosopher, Giambattista Vico (1668-1744) was from Naples and so was Palmer's father, Joseph.

St Louis University is the oldest University west of the Mississippi. It was founded in 1818 by Reverend Louis Guillaume Valentin Dubourg. It is located on Lindell Blvd (Lindell's Grove). It became a Jesuit school in 1827.

Dubourg was Bishop of Louisiana and the Floridas.

Dubourg was born in Haiti and educated in France. Ordained in 1790, he fled France during the revolution in 1792 to exile in Spain. Spain went to war with France in 1793, so Dubourg fled on a ship to Baltimore where his brother had fled to earlier. He was appointed President of Georgetown College on October 1, 1796, serving to 1799. During this time he met George Washington.

Then Dubourg founded St Mary's College (a French College) and ran a lottery to support it. Then he went to

New Orleans as the Apostolic Administrator. On January 8th when the Battle of New Orleans was going on, Dubourg presided at a Mass for American victory over France.

Then Dubourg asked permission to locate his Episcopal See to St Louis, Mo. At that time it was "a kind of miserable barn falling into ruins." When he arrived, he began raising money for a cathedral.

In 1819, Angelo Inglesi, who claimed to be a priest, volunteered his services for St Louis. Dubourg ordained him in 1820 and sent him on a fund raising tour of Europe, along with a request that Inglesi be made coadjutor (financial administrator). He claimed to have raised some money, but the coadjutor job was shot down when he appeared in lay clothes at several social functions in the presence of young women and "exhibited signs of levity and impropriety, both by taking part in dances and by a mode of dress in no way befitting an ecclesiastic". Eventually Dubourg found out that Inglesi was from Quebec, where he married a French Canadian Catholic girl in a Presbyterian Church, then left her for another woman. He was a play director and left Canada just ahead of the bill collectors. (Sound familiar? Like Palmer Rockey!!)

CPSIA information can be obtained at www.ICGtesting.com
Printed in the USA
LVOW12s1733070314

376491LV00002B/442/P